LOVE IN THE LATER YEARS

LOVE IN THE LATER YEARS

The Emotional, Physical, Sexual and Social Potential of the Elderly

by
JAMES A. PETERSON
and
BARBARA PAYNE

ASSOCIATION PRESS / NEW YORK

LOVE IN THE LATER YEARS

International Standard Book Number: 0-8096-1898-2
Library of Congress Catalog Card Number: 75-5839

Library of Congress Cataloging in Publication Data

Peterson, James Alfred.
Love in the later years.

Includes index.
1. Aged—United States. 2. Marriage. 3. Aged—
Sexual behavior. 4. Retirement. I. Payne,
Barbara, joint author. II. Title.
HQ1064.U5P48   301.43′5   75-5839
ISBN 0-8096-1898-2

PRINTED IN THE UNITED STATES OF AMERICA

CONTENTS

PREFACE

In 1900 there were only three million older persons in the United States. They comprised a very small percentage of the population, and, as a result, society paid them little attention. In a youth-centered culture whose great thrust and theme was productivity the generation past sixty was a bother if not an actual embarrassment. Today, when there are nearly 22,000,000 persons above sixty-five with a growing sense of identity and with sharp demands for meaningful lives, many disciplines are beginning to focus research and analysis on their potentials. The result of this research has been to discover that almost all of our views of older persons are destructive myths. Myths which have tended to erode the hopes of older persons for their last years and to stultify society's positive response to them.

No greater myth exists than that which assumes that older persons have no capacity for tender love or sexual response. This myth has touched the quite normal interaction of older persons with the brush of ridicule and thus inhibited guidance for them. It has also blocked the senior citizens in our midst from seeking love. Part of the task of this book is to destroy the myths and to face realistically the problems encountered by older persons as they strive for as full an emotional and intimate life as possible. So far as we know this is the first book to attempt to codify research in this area and to offer a foundation for love in the later years in psychological understanding and care analysis. It will certainly not be the last, however, because our country is moving more and more toward an older population. We are increasingly aware that inevitably we, too, shall have a chance to make our last years the best years.

1

The Later Years in Fresh Perspective

The course of love in the later years is no smoother for older persons than it is for young adults or middle-aged persons. Hearts are broken and dreams dashed at sixty as well as at sixteen. As the decades pass, we may grow in years but we do not seem to grow in mastering love. Furthermore, each age has its own peculiar problems and one's earlier experience is sometimes a poor guide. Also, cultural or social expectations often seem aimed at destroying later love. Romance may be viewed as a jewel of great price in the twenties, but somehow seems ridiculous in the sixties. A great sex life is now regarded to be almost as necessary for the good life as success in the first half of life, but unthinkable as a value for the last half. So prejudice and ignorance conspire to deny older persons satisfaction in their need for intimacy and response. In this book we marshal research and case studies to destroy the myths and to validate love in the later years.

We learn from others. Ben Hurtz helped us understand some of the common difficulties that beset older lovers, in the following case history from our clinic.

Mr. Ben Hurtz presented himself as a neat, intelligent, achieving man of 64 years of age. He was so anxious and agitated that he had difficulty staying in his chair during his first interview. His presenting complaint was a rather sudden but complete impotence. The condition was nine months old when he presented himself to the clinic. His incapacity had now become an obsession . . . he could think of little else. When he talked about his problem he referred to it with much circumlocution, saying: "My problem is that I am growing old." He had been, and was, a highly successful businessman who had built a large business and raised a family of four children who were now all gone from the home. Some gentle probing revealed that his marriage and family life had been rewarding and that until the previous year he had enjoyed a sustained and rewarding erotic relationship with an ardent wife. She was still interested, but he could not satisfy her; in fact, he could not achieve an erection.

It was interesting that the onset of his impotence had coincided with a formal meeting with his superiors at which time his retirement at sixty-five was anticipated. He saw no relationship between these events, but he had reacted to this conference strenuously and had subsequently embarked on a forced program of dieting, exercise and intermittent planning for his retirement. It was no surprise that during this regime he had experienced an episode of impotence which confirmed his earlier fears that he was in fact "growing old." He reacted to the impotence, as he had to the discussion of his retirement, with extreme anxiety. The anxiety forced him to try intercourse over and over again with growing alarm each time he failed. He soon visited his doctor who pronounced him "as fit as he could be at his age" and thus unwittingly added to Ben's growing anxiety.

This state of alarm led him to contemplate many kinds of solutions. His secretary had been divorced several years before and she made no secret of her attachment to him. He was sure that she would have been more than willing to help him solve his problem of "growing old." When he was asked why he had not availed himself of this "help" he said: "If I had failed with her, I would know for sure that I was through, and I didn't want to face that!"

His impotence preyed on his mind so that he made some stupid mistakes at work and tormented his wife at home. He finally sought therapy. His wife was immediately involved, and she proved, fortunately, to be a very understanding female. Further physiology tests were made and they confirmed the original diagnosis . . . if Ben had problems they had little to do with any aging process. Treatment consisted of a great deal of honest exploration about Ben's fears of aging, his reaction to his coming retirement, and about some of his fearfully held myths about the sexuality of older persons. In the meantime his wife was most understanding, and full of devotion and tenderness. The results were positive. Ben dealt with his trauma regarding retirement, and its threat to his self-esteem. He dealt with his long-defensed fears of aging and dying, and he came again to trust his wife and to respect her profound love for him. They re-established their communication and their expressions of affection. It was then no great surprise that they came one day to announce that they would not be back.

The themes that run through this case study are love, trust, fear, anxiety, sex and self-esteem. These themes will intermingle in many ways in this book. It is, of course, noteworthy that for the first time in the history of man it is important to recount the problems of a couple at 64 years of age. Because, again for the first time, many marriages are persisting into old age. Until seventy years ago marriage was almost inevitably terminated by the death of one or the other partner in mid-life. The average life span then was forty-seven years. A marriage rarely lasted long enough to permit both partners to witness the departure of all the children from home. A visit to an old cemetery is very instructive. The span of life was brief.

Today millions of men and women are in marriages that may last fifteen to twenty years beyond middle age. This is a new and very novel phenomenon. It is an opportunity seldom before accorded to any human beings. So we have no models, no role definitions for such older wives and husbands. In a sense they are pioneers. Where there are so many people facing an undefined future, it is important to marshal as much insight as possible for their guidance. Many of them are not doing very well in their exploration of this unknown terrain. Many are giving up in middle age or soon after. Most observers agree that the divorce rate for these couples is rising at a phenomenal rate. Comparative statistical data on this point are fragmentary. In March of 1974, however, the Bureau of the Census determined that in the preceding four years the divorce rate had increased as much as it had in the previous ten years. While the general pattern still holds that the majority of divorces are obtained in the earlier years of marriage, no age group has thus far remained immune from the rising rate of divorce. As Figure 1 makes clear, even marriages of twenty-five years' duration are no longer secure. We know something about their problems from research and from case studies. We will analyze that material as closely as possible in this book so that such couples can have at their disposal as much information as possible to use to cope with their exploration of love in the later years.

A quick look at the figures on marital status in the later years is instructive and, in one sense, will define some of the problems that must be faced. In March of 1971 there were some 11,000,000 mar-

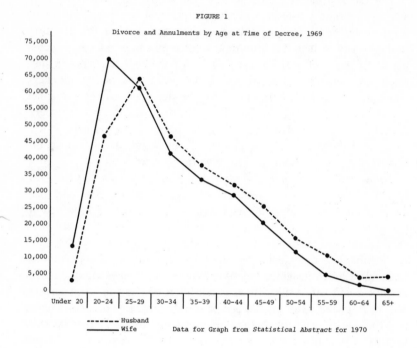

FIGURE 1

Divorce and Annulments by Age at Time of Decree, 1969

------- Husband
——— Wife   Data for Graph from *Statistical Abstract* for 1970

ried couples who were over 55 years of age. Six million of them were over 65. But death had already disrupted many unions so that at the same time there were some 8,300,000 widows and some 1,700,000 widowers. In addition to the widows and widowers there were 1,000,-000 divorced women and 500,000 divorced men who had not re-married. Thus, in addition to the 22,000,000 married persons there were 11,500,000 who were either widowed or divorced, without a mate, and generally living alone. So one half of those over 55 years of age had no companion for their later years.

It is obvious from these figures that the single older women outnumber the single men by a huge majority. There is a plurality of females of some 7,000,000. Putting it another way, there are four times as many single women as men. It is for this reason that we title this book *Love in the Later Years* rather than follow the example of its immediate predecessor, which was titled *Married Love in the Middle Years*. We must not neglect almost half of the older people.

Thus, this book has two major thrusts: one is the discussion of the problems and opportunities of the 22,000,000 older persons who are married during these years; and the second is directed to the problems and alternatives of the 11,500,000 single persons over 55 years of age. We will look at the peculiar strains in their relationships due to physical, psychological, economic and sexual difficulties that are unique to the later years. We will look at the degree of interdependence and interstimulation in their marriages and see to what degree these couples have succumbed to a placid indifference to each other and why they are more prone to divorce than were their parents. More important, we will describe specific models and examples of adjustment styles that seem to make the final twenty years the *harvest years* of tenderness and creative achievement.

We are convinced that most of the difficulties of men and women, and marriage, in the later years are due to the pernicious influence of myths. Older people tend to give up satisfactions because the myths say they cannot have those satisfactions. They often are indolent mentally because they have been brainwashed to think they have no brains. They rock in a chair because they are placed there by the false expectations of society. They are sexually impotent or frigid because the generation of their children were taught that there is something demeaning in sex for older persons. One by one these myths have been destroyed by research, but their destructive power hangs on. We hope this book can marshal the evidence that marital life can be rich for those 11,000,000 married couples, and thus point the way for them to use their final quarter century creatively and lovingly.

However, we must not neglect the 11,500,000 older persons who are not married. Most surveys studying the major problems of aging persons have found one problem that is always near the top of the list; it is the problem of loneliness. Loneliness is associated with poor morale, inadequate mental health, and withdrawal from creativity.

Marie Calendar is 62 years old. Her husband, Jack, died of a massive brain hemorrhage five years ago, after they had been married for thirty-one years. Jack was a plumbing contractor who had started his firm just after the building boom began in the post-World War II years. He made the most of his opportunities and developed one of the most successful firms in the Middle West. But that success took its toll from his marriage and from his health. Jack was a great financial success but a failure as a husband and a father.

Consequently his son and daughter left home early and were involved in a series of hasty and disastrous marriages. One drifted east and the other west and before Jack's death, both had disappeared. Marie stayed on but only as a nursemaid to her husband in their last decade together.

When Jack died it was both a relief and a blow to Marie. She was relieved because Jack had never been a husband and it was a blow because as nurse she had few friends or relationships. What she did have was remarkable health and optimism. She looked like a 41-year-old woman and she felt she could offer a great deal to a second husband for her remaining twenty or thirty years.

But now her optimism is gone. She says the only men she has met are frustrated married males or exploitative single men who know she is secure financially. They offer companionship but with a price tag. They all want her to invest in their projects. No one seems interested in Marie—only in Marie in bed or at the bank.

Marie had thirty-one years of a disastrous marriage and now has had five years of disillusionment. She is ready to give up. But once in a while she accepts a date because she still has a glimmering hope that given the opportunity, she could make up for thirty-one years of misery.

When Marie came to us for counseling her depression was full blown. She wanted to know what chances there were at her age for a normal, rewarding relationship. We had heard the same question from eight attractive widows the day before on a cable television panel. What chances? When there are four or five times the number of women to men? And when men age sexually more rapidly than women?

What are the chances in our society that these 11,500,000 persons can find some warm companionship, some intimacy, in such a situation? Some of them are embarking on late-life marriages popularly characterized as "retirement marriage." Have these unions prospered and what guidelines are there to ensure greater success for them? Others have retreated to single sex groups; while still others have experimented by moving into communes. Some have entered retirement communities, and still others have begun to practice a new form of polygamy. If love is the hallmark of contentedness at any age we need to assess these and other alternatives for older single persons.

It is important, too, to understand what the future holds in terms of demographic trends. There is some indication that as women enter into leadership and executive positions in society their life span will drop to much more nearly equal that of men. Thus an equal place in society may tend to equalize the male and female ratio during the later years. However, this may take one hundred years, and there are indications that middle-age and older unions are failing at an unprecedented rate, with many more individuals thus being shunted into single status for their later years. The divorce rate for persons after the age of 55 has doubled in the last ten years. It is of course much easier for the male to find a new mate than for the female. What can we make of these trends for our needs of tomorrow? We will try to untangle the implications of all these processes and come to some tentative conclusions as to the future of later-day marriages before we are finished. Even more important will be some basic insights regarding the avoidance of the conditions that lead to marital dissolution.

This is a book of sociological, psychological and human analysis. We cannot be content with descriptions of ideal and often inappropriate examples. We have tried to help real people in real situations for over thirty years. Our recommendations thus come out of living with these problems with real people. We plan to probe into the background factors of health, nutrition, exercise, sexual capacity, personality change, family relationships, and intellectual promise so that couples studying this book will be aware of their potential in any loving relationship. What is current is not necessarily normative—that is, the present marital situation may not represent all that is possible or that might be. A mere description of what studies and cases indicate is not enough and this book is not simply a report. We look at current research from the point of view of potentialities.

If it were necessary we could insert at this point a hundred case studies to show how older persons have beaten the odds—how they have discovered that the "second time around" can be rewarding and fulfilling. We won't do that, however, because the rest of our book proves the point. One of the great new words in gerontological research is *hope*. We believe in that! There is hope and potential for every person over 60 years of age to find a new intimacy and fulfillment. This will take investment and involvement, but it is quite possible.

Consequently this is a book that, while based on research, moves toward hope. In this sense much that has been learned in gerontological research and in our case studies is germane as we think about love in the later years. Many older people are finding and enjoying love in their maturity. This is not a quest without obstacles, however, but we would not write unless we thought that for the first time in history there is hope these later years can be magnificent. Potentialities are steppingstones to fulfillment. What happens to you depends on how you respond!

2

Myth and Reality About Marriage and Love in the Later Years

A great many persons regard the relationship of older persons with a certain wry sense of amusement. This reflects the widely held attitude of younger persons that romance, devotion and sex have little relevance to the lives of individuals past the age of 55. The couplet that goes "Come, grow old with me/The best is yet to be" is usually regarded only as a sentimental delusion. Older persons are viewed as intellectually decrepit, sexually indifferent and physically crippled. The wise older person is supposedly one who abandons the zest and sentiment of his younger years and subsides in an unobtrusive manner into a passionless oblivion.

These social expectations are not lost on the older citizens. They serve to become guides for expectations. So the older person consequently defines his activity in terms of retreat and obscurity. The reason the Gray Panthers (an emerging activist movement of religiously oriented older persons) and their leader, Marjorie Kuhn, are controversial is because they challenge that stereotype. There is something disturbing about lambs turning into panthers. The negative attitude toward the political life of older persons is only part of a more general attitude of abandonment and depreciation of the elderly.

This self-fulfilling view of older persons has done untold damage in inhibiting the life satisfactions of these older persons. When there were only a few persons beyond the age of 55 it did not matter so much. But now, when we look at the fact that within two decades half of the population of the nation will be over 50 years of age, we realize that we are dealing with the potential happiness of millions of people. It thus becomes important to expose the myths that destroy people and to maximize the efforts that may liberate them. Those older persons are not all cut on the same historical bias, and they do not have the same potentials. Indeed, they differ in many ways, as we will discover on closer inspection.

Mental Capacity

Several years ago a young couple made an appointment to see us at our clinic. They proved to be a brother and sister. They had no sibling conflict; instead, their concern was their 68-year-old father. The girl (Betty) said:

> We are troubled about Dad. He's doing strange things. Mother has been dead nine years. She always was a good balance for Dad. Now he must be getting senile. He's dating and staying out to all hours. When my 14-year-old insisted on long hair Dad sided with him. He says he's begun to question just how good God really is. We really fear he's getting childish. We wonder if all older persons lose their brains. Should we think of an institution for Dad.

A great many persons have accepted the myth that all older persons inevitably become simpleminded and irresponsible. Of course it was very convenient for Betty to blame senility for the attitudes her father exhibited that didn't match hers. She wanted him to be a docile and dependent person, but after the repressive mother died he turned out to be a modern and lively person. We involved the whole family in group therapy and Dad emerged as easily the most intelligent and wisest person of them all.

Do older persons inevitably become "simpleminded"? The results of dozens of responsible studies show just the opposite. The vast majority of our seniors grow in mental acuity and practical wisdom as they grow older. K. Warner Schaie has devoted most of his life to researching this problem. One study involved 301 subjects, ranging in age from 21 to 70, over a period of seven years. In this study he found that there is no change over the years in *cognitive flexibility* which means the ability to shift from one way of thinking to another and there is a systematic increase in scores for *crystallized intelligence* which means inductive reasoning, verbal comprehension and numerical skills.

So older persons can be trusted in human relations. They are neither intellectually dull nor morally irresponsible. If anything, they are wiser in love than are their adolescent grandchildren. We shall review in a later chapter the success of retirement marriages. There the wisdom of choice and success in these later marriages will be clearly seen. Of course, in a small number of cases a few older men or women who are mentally incompetent have been exploited. The press has done its share in making us keenly aware of these cases. But for each such case there are thousands of successful marital ventures.

Most of us will retain and sharpen our critical mental faculties all through our senior years. There was no more reason for Betty to question her father's sanity than to question her own. The idea of brain deterioration with age is really a savage myth which has operated to destroy the independence and happiness of millions of older persons.

Physical Decline

Betty didn't stress her father's physical problems in her visit at the clinic. She was wise, because her father was physically (and emotionally) healthier than she was. But another daughter (40-year-old Helen) did—with vehemence. She expostulated:

Dad can't get married! He's 70 years old. He's got problems handling his life now without adding all the problems of marriage. He goes out with that woman and comes back looking so tired. You have to help us prevent this thing from happening.

When, later, I got the daughter and the father together to discuss the situation, it was clear that she had a totally unwarranted concern about her father's health. He had regular health examinations that showed him to be fit as a fiddle and perfectly capable of marriage. Throughout the interview Helen kept saying, "But Dad, you are old, and you never know what can happen tomorrow."

Her father was a patient man but he finally ended the argument by saying: "No, no one knows what will happen tomorrow. That's all the more reason to be happy today! I'm going to get married."

As a matter of fact, her father was right. The majority of older persons are in good health, fully able to cope with a new partner and to enjoy a new sexual experience with that partner. Figure 2, based on a graph developed by Fisher and Birren, makes it clear that strength in a wide variety of the body's muscles decreases very slowly

FIGURE 2

Relationship of Strength to Age

(Values are plotted as a percentage of the maximum. Each curve is drawn to a different base line, separated by 20 percentage points from the next)

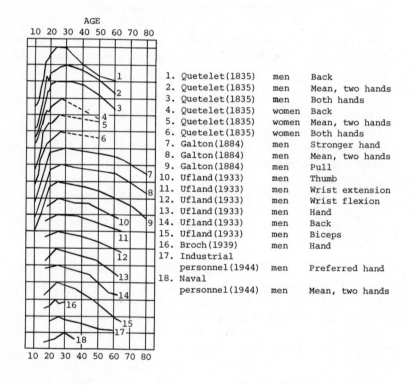

1. Quetelet(1835)	men	Back
2. Quetelet(1835)	men	Mean, two hands
3. Quetelet(1835)	men	Both hands
4. Quetelet(1835)	women	Back
5. Quetelet(1835)	women	Mean, two hands
6. Quetelet(1835)	women	Both hands
7. Galton(1884)	men	Stronger hand
8. Galton(1884)	men	Mean, two hands
9. Galton(1884)	men	Pull
10. Ufland(1933)	men	Thumb
11. Ufland(1933)	men	Wrist extension
12. Ufland(1933)	men	Wrist flexion
13. Ufland(1933)	men	Hand
14. Ufland(1933)	men	Back
15. Ufland(1933)	men	Biceps
16. Broch(1939)	men	Hand
17. Industrial personnel(1944)	men	Preferred hand
18. Naval personnel(1944)	men	Mean, two hands

SOURCE: Birren, James A. and M. Bruce Fisher, *Journal of Applied Psychology,* Vol. 31, p. 490, 1947. Reprinted by permission of the American Psychology Association, Washington, D.C.

in maturity (see Figure 2). After the fifth decade, to be sure, strength decreases at somewhat greater rate. But even at the age of 60 years the loss does not usually exceed 10 to 20 per cent of the maximum. There simply is no physical basis for denying older persons the comfort of companionship and love.

Marital Happiness in the Later Years: A Declining Curve

While the evidence for continuing mental and physical health seems clear, the fact remains that most major research studies of the adjustment of marital pairs at mid-life indicate that in the vast majority of cases the marriage has traveled a long way on the road to disintegration by the time a couple reach their mid-fifties.

There are several research strategies available for determining the relationship between duration and marital adjustment. The most valid method would be to follow a sufficient number of couples through the various phases of their family cycle—studying them at the inception of marriage and then interviewing them at stated intervals thereafter. If those interviewing intervals coincided with the various developmental phases of their life cycle, the results would provide an invaluable mosaic of changing structures, roles and family processes. This has yet to be done, however. The closest approximation has been the Burgess and Wallin study in which couples were interviewed during engagement, three to five years later, and then again after they had been married for up to twenty years. The first phase sample had 1,000 couples, the second had 666 couples, and the third consisted of 400 respondent couples. The results in terms of gain or loss of adjustment in the third stage are shown in Figure 3. Peter C. Pineo, who compiled the table used in Figure 3, chooses the word *disenchantment* to describe the magnitude of loss of adjustment. He does not feel that the phrase *loss of satisfaction* is semantically powerful enough to indicate the overwhelming drop in almost every phase of interaction. Certainly such pervasive disenchantment during middle age is not grounds on which to predict great contributions to the mate or to the marriage in the retirement years.

However predictive the Burgess and Wallin study may be of poverty in later interaction it does not yet give us information as to what actually happens to these disenchanted couples. Do they overcome their disillusionment or does it deepen? A second study, made by Blood and Wolfe does give some good information about disenchantment trends. They present a view of 556 urban and rural families in

FIGURE 3

Changes in Marital Adjustment from Early to Middle
Years of Marriage on 18 Indices — 400 Couples

	Change from Early to Middle Years	
	Husbands	Wives
MARITAL SATISFACTION		
Marital adjustment	-4.63*	-5.42*
Love	-2.01*	-2.87*
Permanence	-2.12*	-2.64*
Consensus	-2.26*	-2.37*
Marriage complaints (absence of)	-1.59	-2.09*
Own happiness	-1.13	-1.42
Sexual adjustment	-1.14	-0.93
MARITAL TYPE		
Sharing of interests and activities	-3.84*	-4.56*
Frequency of sexual intercourse	-2.31*	-2.13*
Traditionalism	-1.86	-0.76
Attitudes to having children	-0.04	-0.72
Dominance	-0.79	-0.26
PERSONAL CHARACTERISTICS		
Idealization of mate's personality	-0.60	-0.67
Personal growth gains due to marriage	-0.16	-0.36
Non-neuroticism or autonomy	-0.24	-0.12
Rating of own personality traits	-1.07	-0.34
Rating of mate's personality traits	0.34	-1.31
Number of felt personality needs	1.45	1.25

SOURCE: Pineo, Peter c. "Disenchantment in the Later Years of
Marriage," *Journal of Marriage and the Family,* February, 1961,
p.4. Reprinted by permission

NOTE: A "minus" sign indicates a loss in that aspect of the
relationship. An asterisk indicates changes large enough to
be statistically significant, i.e., not due to chance.

different life stages by means of interviewing families in various stages of the life cycle. They did not follow one group of marriages through time, but rather studied different age segments at the same time to make a synthetic family-life-cycle history. This study loses the authenticity which results from following the same persons, but it gains in scope so that older persons are included in this study. As the study was based on an excellently designed sample it has a better social-class distribution than does the study done by Burgess and Wallin. It profits by the inclusion of a lower socio-economic group of respondents, making it more representative. We are again interested in the course of marital adjustment as related to duration of the marriage since this tests the capacity of the marriage relationship to offer resources of satisfaction to the aging husband or wife. The findings of this study regarding marital satisfaction and duration of marriage are summarized in Figure 4.

FIGURE 4

Marital Satisfaction by Duration of the Marriage

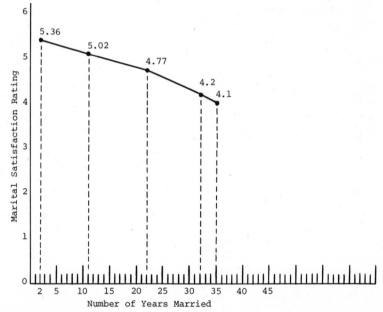

SOURCE: Blood, Robert O., Jr., and Donald M. Wolfe, *Husbands and Wives: The Dynamics of Married Living*, 1960. Reprinted by permission of the Macmillan Company, New York, N.Y.

It is obvious that the same degree of change noted in Pineo's study of disenchantment is reported here. Blood and Wolfe conclude (more directly than Pineo) that time has a *corrosive* influence on marriage. After twenty years or longer, only 6 per cent of the respondent wives were *fully satisfied* with marriage. In summarizing the study, Leslie says, "Middle-aged people find satisfaction in children, in jobs, in their friends, and elsewhere, but they seldom find much satisfaction in each other." This is a stark conclusion and we will test it by other studies.

Blood and Wolfe carry their analysis of interaction on the level of the fate of marital love and companionship into the retirement years. Figure 5 indicates that the trends of dissatisfaction with marital adjustment in middle age are not reversed later.

FIGURE 5

Wife's Satisfaction with Love and
Companionship by Stage in Family Life Cycle

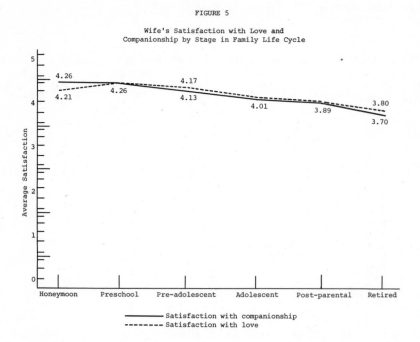

SOURCE: Blood, Robert O., Jr., and Donald M. Wolfe, *Husbands and Wives: The Dynamics of Married Living*, 1960. Reprinted by permission of the Macmillan Company, New York, N.Y.

The major explanation for this corrosive nature of time and the correlation between duration of marriage and disenchantment seems to lie in the fact couples tend to do less together as the married years go on. They carve out individual careers in which there is an accompanying loss of shared role tasks and an accentuation of role specialization. They have less in common and do more and more in a solo manner. Figure 6 represents this trend graphically. The inference is that as husband and wife age they no longer either need or can use the help and advice of their mate.

A third study confirms the process of alienation that is suggest-

FIGURE 6

Role Specialization by Stage in Family Life Cycle

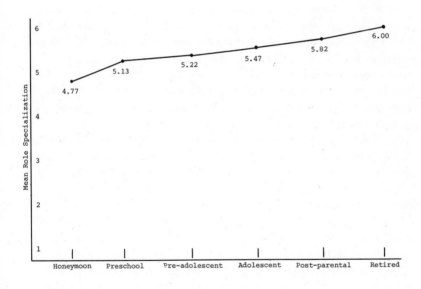

SOURCE: Blood, Robert O., Jr., and Donald M. Wolfe, *Husbands and Wives: The Dynamics of Married Living,* 1960. Reprinted by permission of the Macmillan Company, New York, N.Y.

ed by the concept of role specialization. We noted that the data from
Blood and Wolfe were welcome because of the information from the
lower socio-economic group. This third study involved upper-middle
and lower-upper marriages and may be added to the two studies already reviewed in order to cover all socio-economic classes and give
some adequate representation to all groups. Cuber and Harroff studied
in depth 437 persons who were highly educated and financially successful. Their study is appropriately titled, *The Significant Americans*.
This study was done in different style, for it does not depend on quan-
titative norms but rather on interview material. Cuber and Harroff
were able to distinguish sharp differences in type of marital style of
these middle-aged and late-middle-aged men and women. This study
is discussed here as a third indicator of our general conclusion that
within marriage there is little support from the other for the aging
husband or wife.

Cuber and Harroff's first category is that of the *Conflict-Habit-
uated Relationship*. This is characterized by a great deal of tension
and conflict. "Incompatibility is pervasive and conflict is ever potential." The second group is named the *Devitalized Relationships*. These
marriages are "apathetic, lifeless." The third group is labeled the *Passive-Congenial Relationship*. In this there is very little conflict, for
they are passively content and not disillusioned, "even though they
show so little vitality and so little evidence that the spouse is important
—much less indispensable—to the satisfaction they say they enjoy."

The fourth group has *Vital Relationships*. The characteristics are
vitality, vibrancy, and the "excited sharing of some important life experience." Both the husband and wife sacrifice other satisfactions for
their relationship and find significance in the importance of their
union. This is a small group.

The last group has *Total Relationships* which are vital and vi-
brant. All important aspects of life are "mutually shared and enthu-
siastically participated in."

No statistical analysis is presented, but the inference is that the
vast majority of their respondents fell in the first three conflict-ridden
or dead categories of marriages.

The Birren *et al.* study of 47 men devoted a section to an analysis of marital and family relationships.

Husband and wife rapport was identified as falling in one of four
categories:

—good and improved in old age,

—continued compatible or workable,

—continued poor,

—deteriorated in old age from either compatible or poor earlier relationship.

The authors comment that "about one third of the men were rated as having poor and often deteriorating relationships with their wives" and that "among the two thirds described as compatible, there was a broad range—from satisfying relationships to mere ragged compatibility." If we relate this study to the others we would include those with "ragged compatibility" with the *passive-congenial* or *devitalized*. In this study it is perhaps fair to say that in at least 50 per cent of the cases there is little ground for believing that the relationship is vital enough on any level of intimacy to add meaning and support to either the husband or wife.

Lowenthal provides further insight into the failure of contemporary marital interaction to provide depth of emotional response. Her study is based on 280 "sample survivors" who were drawn on a stratified-random basis from eighteen San Francisco census tracts and interviewed three times at annual intervals. She found that "an individual who has been widowed within seven years, and who has a confidant, has even higher morale than a person who remains married but lacks a confidant." Her findings carry the clear implication (see Fig. 7) that *a marital partner in old age has lost some ability and motivation to offer intimacy or emotional support* to his or her mate. We assume that the 47 per cent satisfaction rating for marrieds without a confidant in contrast to the 27 per cent satisfaction rating for widowed without a confidant implies that the San Francisco sample includes (as did the Cuber sample) some *vital* relationships which supply closeness, and that they are comparable in terms of outcomes. But the value of a constant companion is also evident in this study. Older persons who are married live longer, have better mental and emotional health and are less lonely. Yet the inevitable conclusion of this study is that a great many married persons have little intimacy to support them in later days. The study shows contemporary American marriages to be marked by either disillusionment, conflict or devitalization.

An Emerging Marital Style

It must be noted, however, that other studies have challenged these negative descriptions of marital happiness in the middle years.

FIGURE 7

Effect of Confidant on Morale in Widowhood,
Retirement and Physical Illness N=280

	Satisfied (per cent)	Depressed (per cent)
WIDOWED WITHIN 7 YEARS		
Has confidant	55	45
No confidant	27	73
MARRIED		
Has confidant	65	35
No confidant	47	53
RETIRED WITHIN 7 YEARS		
Has confidant	50	50
No confidant	36	64
NOT RETIRED		
Has confidant	70	30
No confidant	50	50
SERIOUS PHYSICAL ILLNESS WITHIN 2 YEARS		
Has confidant	16	84
No confidant	13	87
NO SERIOUS ILLNESS		
Has confidant	64	36
No confidant	42	58

Source: Lowenthal, Marjorie Fiske, and Clayton Haven, "Interaction and Adaptation: Intimacy as a Critical Variable," *American Sociological Review*, February 1968, Vol. 33, no. 1, p. 27. Reprinted by permission of the American Sociological Association.

Peterson found a great deal of mutual dependence and stability in 500 couples with an average age of 62 in the retirement community he studied. He reported that the married group was the happiest of any in the community; that most of the problems were settled by give-and-take and that the happiness score would compare well with any other age group.

Feldman and Rollins report on various aspects of marriage in terms of each stage of the family life cycle in a study of 240 couples titled "Marital Satisfaction Over the Family Life Cycle." They found that general satisfaction increases after middle age and during the period of retirement. They also found, however, that "positive companionship experiences with their spouses at least once a day or more often" decrease during the life cycle of most marriages and reach a low point during retirement. The events used to measure companionship are "laughing together, calm discussions with each other, having a stimulating exchange of ideas with each other, and working on a project." These are measurable items and together form a scale that is used to depict the degree of companionship during the various stages of the life cycle. The graph in Figure 8 shows what happens to companionship as measured by these items.

Burr's study is limited by a small sample with only eleven couples in the post-parental group and only ten couples in the retired group. But, even so, analysis of the sample shows no decline in satisfaction over the total cycle of marriage.

While the evidence is not unequivocal, it is probably fair to say that a great many marriages approach the retirement stage of the family life cycle stale and dreary. This overwhelming fact cannot be ignored. There are an increasing number of both marriages and divorces occurring after age 45, when the children leave. At that time many partners seem to have lost life satisfaction, sexual communication, verbal interchange, their role sharing, and no longer are stimulating to each other. This is not universally true, however. Always, in the statistics of these studies, there were some couples far above the norm of disenchantment or corrosion. For some the marital union grows closer and more cherished. All of this seems to suggest that given some planning and some effort, marriage can grow in meaning as the years pass. It is probable in our society that both partners must invest a great deal in the marital enterprise if it is to thrive and not to shrivel.

As a matter of fact, this probably means that we are witnessing

FIGURE 8

Positive Companionship Experiences with Their Spouses

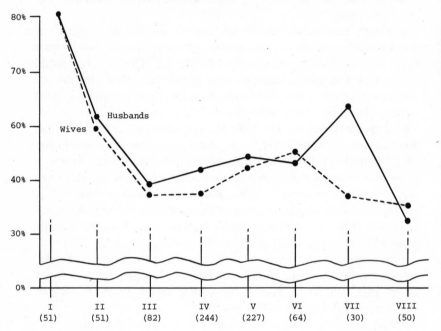

SOURCE: Rollins, Boyd C. and Harold Feldman, "Marital Satisfaction
Over Family Life Cycle," Journal of Marriage and the Family, Feb.
1970, Vol. 32, no. I, p. 20. Reprinted by permission.

the emergence of a new era so far as the marriage relationship is concerned. In our grandparents' day, when marriage was often terminated
early and abruptly, economic pressures were so great, the use of human instead of mechanical energy so necessary, that little time or attention could be given to either personality development or to the marital union itself. What we are now witnessing is a new type of marriage which has both greater fragility and greater promise. Given
economic affluence, leisure time, and more education both men and
women are demanding far greater returns from their relationships. If
the marriage is not productive, divorce is an easy alternative. Soaring

divorce rates indicate that a great many couples are finding earlier marriages inadequate, so they try again. This does not mean the demise of marriage. A greater proportion of the population is marrying today, and more often! This may seem to be a trend toward disorganization, but, on the other hand, it can well be a testimony to the emerging expectation that life should be rewarding and exciting. The problem seems to be how to make marriage to the same person exciting and stimulating over a period of years. Failing in this, more and more people are trying again with another partner.

Certainly physical and emotional health is a major prerequisite to the rich interaction of men and women in later years. We are in the process of learning much about psychological states during the later years. Some studies have indicated that the female who stays home as mother and homemaker is much more susceptible to mental illness than is her counterpart who combines homemaking with an outside career. There are other studies which show that the married person has more stability than the widowed or the divorced. We now have enough data on which to develop some guidelines for good mental health in the years after age 55.

We are aware that the decline of sexuality or sexual capacity due to age is a myth. We know that it is possible through good nutrition, exercise and preventive medicine to maintain top-notch health during the later years. We know that the human mind does not fade gradually into senility. The older husband and wife with proper health regimes and mental stimulation can match younger persons who are in their thirties and forties.

It is not enough to destroy the myths about older persons, however. It is necessary to institute both physical and mental health programs so that there is an adequate physical and psychological platform for zestful marital living. But, given the best of physical and mental health, there are still interactional difficulties in later relationships. In the next chapter we will turn to the specific analysis of various problems for the groups we have specified and we will also look at sensible ways of meeting these problems and enriching the relationships themselves.

3

Making the Most of the Later Years of Marriage

Beyond the achievement of good physical and mental health there are necessary role changes and adjustments which must be part of marital adjustment. This is indicated by scientific studies which show that even for healthy couples the gradual drop in marital adjustment begun during the early years of marriage continues, eventually reaching its lowest point in the retirement years. Sexual adjustment scores show a similar decrease in this period. The wife's score of satisfaction with her husband reaches a low point in this period. Roles are threatened, with the husband reaching a low point of power in the relationship as soon as he retires.

For these marital adjustment problems in the later years to be analyzed most fruitfully, it seems important to develop a typology of such marriages. The most common approach has probably been to look at the particular problems of those who are in their fifties, sixties, seventies or eighties. The difficulty with such an approach lies in the fact that age is no real measure of aging! Some seventy-year-olds are far more alive than some fifty-year-olds. Chronological aging alone is a poor measure of physiological or psychological conditions.

It is probable that a typology based on life history is more adequate for understanding. We propose, consequently, to look at the love life of individuals in terms of what has happened to them in their marital relationships. We propose the following typology as important

in thinking clearly about love problems in the later years. The following types seem to discriminate between radically different life or marital histories:

1. Those marriages which were contracted early, before twenty-
   five, and which have persisted into the late years and which have
   a duration of thirty or more years; *and* those marriages which
   were contracted after a first marriage but before age 35.

2. Those marriages which were contracted during middle age (between age 40 and 60) after the first marriage was broken by
   divorce or by death.

3. Those marriages (known as "retirement marriages") which were
   contracted after age 60.

This typology was developed because it seems to us that a couple
who have lived together for forty years have essentially different expectations and problems from a couple who married in their middle
years, after one or more earlier marriages. And both of these couples
are clearly different from the "retirement marriage" couple. One difficulty with much of the previous analysis of remarriage has been that
it has not always observed this differentiation. These days, however,
the increased incidence of middle-age divorce and remarriage makes
such a typology indispensable if we are to deal adequately with love
in the later years.

There are, of course, other variables which must be considered. If
there are children involved in a relationship, we cannot overlook what
that fact does. On the other hand, if there are no children, we cannot
overlook what that fact does, either. If the female has worked at outside employment for her whole life, there is a different meaning attached to widowhood, divorce or remarriage in her case. If one or
the other of a couple is not in good health or is immobilized, this must
make some change in relationship. All the "intervening variables"
such as these must be added to the life-history situation defined by
our typology. This makes the analysis more difficult, but it also makes
it more meaningful.

The Adjustment of First Marriages Persisting Into Old Age

Surprisingly the adjustment problems of those who have been
married thirty or more years and never divorced may be more severe,
in one sense, than the problems of those who marry during middle

age. This is because habituated life patterns tend to become deeply ingrained after thirty years. When retirement comes and roles are threatened, power balances shift, communication decreases, and there may not be enough flexibility and adaptability to accommodate these shifts. These are the marriages that are devitalized and dull.

One basic problem is the need to adjust to the loss of role identity which the male suffers on retirement. In our society a man's self-esteem depends largely on what he accomplishes in and by his work. He loses power with his wife when he gives that up. He also gives up the total life-style of going to work, having camaraderie with his fellow workers, associating with them in a union or a club, incessantly discussing work problems with them, and then going home to relax and rest. Now he is at home twenty-four hours a day. He may play golf or walk, but he is constantly around the house. It is often said by disconsolate wives that they married their husbands for dinner but not for lunch. The woman, of course, lost her main occupation—raising her children—long ago. She was forced to make adjustments then to her retirement. But the husband now includes her in his efforts to cope with the unemployment of his time and energy. He wanders around the house. They are both uncertain about goals and meanings in this last phase of the life cycle. Having been socialized by society to believe that the woman's major task is investing in her children and the major task of the male is work, they are both stunned. Their roles have disappeared, their time schedules are shattered, and their economic security is, if not jeopardized, at least threatened. They are strangers to themselves, for they, as producers and creators, have been shunted onto a sidetrack of life to wait for death. Is it so strange that having no answers to share about their individual selves, they find it difficult to enjoy sharing each other? He paces because he has no direction in which to walk, and she complains because the objects of her attention are gone.

Clara and Henry Nesbit were in the third year of their retirement when they came to discuss their problems. Their history revealed a well-adjusted but mediocre marriage. It was well adjusted in the sense that they had met the normal functions of marriage well; they had raised two children, purchased a home, met their financial obligations and planned for sufficient funds to have a comfortable retirement. It was mediocre in the sense that they had never developed any mutual patterns of stimulation or individual patterns of growth. Clara had been content to take care of the house, purchase food and raise children, but had never developed any friendships or outside interests. Her home was her castle and she stayed there. Henry had been content to feed his family and watch sports on television. The fact of retirement did not bother him too much because he had never invested too much in his job or in the community. He vaguely felt that he would develop some interests like fishing or gardening, but he had no experience in doing either.

During Henry's first year of retirement he bought a fishing pole, a spade and garden seeds. He bravely began his retirement career on a nearby lake and in the garden. But the fish didn't bite and the seeds didn't grow. The weeds seemed more enthusiastic than the tomatoes. Not being used to physical labor he began to wonder why all this exertion when he could buy tomatoes at the corner store without all that labor. So he gave up fishing and gardening and began to spend more time in front of the television set. However, he did not like soap operas and his wife was wedded to them. When this resulted in conflict over use of the television set Clara told him he ought to find outside interests and let her have the house and the TV set during the day. He tried wandering around town. He visited pool halls and senior citizen centers, but none of them appealed to him. So he came back home.

Psychologically he was restless and temperamentally he was testy. Clara bought some parlor games but he had never played games and soon gave this up. He grew much too heavy. Clara finally got him to their doctor, who prescribed dieting and exercise. Henry was too apathetic by now to stick with either. Clara became alarmed and began to heckle him. He responded with some bitterness, so long periods of silence grew up between them. He perceived that there was little of value in his life and that he was losing any relationship with Clara. All of this plus his self-hatred at his overweight condition finally made him depressed. He began to speak about his uselessness and his feeling that the world would be just as well off if he were not there.

This prompted Clara to call her minister and he came to visit with Henry. The minister also caught some inkling of Henry's hopelessness and referred him to the clinic. It was at this point that intervention began. All the usual conditions were discovered. When Henry had retired and become inactive and later depressed, he had also become impotent. With the depression came withdrawal and he had avoided both his children and his friends. His life space had become smaller and smaller so that it shut out many possible rewards of retirement.

Clara had been able to fixate her lifelong motherhood role on Henry. He needed her and this gave her a feeling of importance and significance. But she was so anxious about him that her efforts at help were often lacking in imagination and often hostile. Instead of support she was often depreciating. Her inability to help or to understand him was very frustrating and she wept a great deal—an exercise that did not bring out the best in Henry.

Intervention focused at the beginning on Henry's depression, impotence, weight and withdrawal. Clara was a part of every session in order that she could develop some understanding from the therapist about modeling help for her husband as well as dealing with her anxiety. She proved quite willing to cooperate in the rehabilitation of their sexual life and household management. A joint inventory was attempted to try to discover areas where Henry might find some meaning in the last years of his life. Clara and Henry became part of a post-retirement group which was exploring ways of enriching interaction and life-styles. The group was quite responsive to Clara and Henry and showed much concern for them. Clara and Henry also re-established close relations with their children's families and began to enjoy contacts with their grandchildren. When this was reported, members of the post-retirement group urged Clara and Henry to try out the Grandparenting Program. They were reluctant, but they volunteered and both found a great deal of satisfaction in that program. It was about this time that they volunteered to the therapist the feeling that they could now direct the rest of their lives without help and therapy was terminated.

The problem of the substitution of meaningful roles that might substitute for work-life and motherhood roles is difficult enough by itself, but at mid-life the authority roles change, too. When a man comes home with a paycheck—the quickest clue in our culture to a man's status in the outside world—he deserves power and gets it. But when he is roaming around and not producing anything, that which had inspired his wife to admire him and respect him is gone. The depression studies of Cavan, Hill, and Angel agree that when a man lost employment in the Great Depression his prestige disappeared in his family. Something similar happens when he is retired. Now he is more of an equal. There may be another factor in this loss of power on the part of the male. The female knows the statistics about mortality among men and women. She may be bracing herself for widowhood, aware that in a short or longer period of time she must become the guardian of the finances and make her own way. These years may unconsciously be her socialization for widowhood and she may be rehearsing an independence that she will assume when he dies.

It did not matter so much who was boss when the children were young and the wife's chief task was child-raising. But when the children are gone, and she is restless, and the balance of her hormones tilt away from estrogen, she often rises up with determination to de-

mand more say in the relationship. Reuben Hill's study of family power allotments across three generations seems to indicate that this is
true (see Figure 9). He found that in the grandparents of his sample,
the patterns of authority centered in the woman was the one which appeared most frequently.

The part of this report by objective observers is quite interesting
because one would have supposed that the grandfather cohort, made
up certainly of a generation that had never heard of Women's Lib,
would not enter their last phase of life with the woman dominant in
more cases than the male.

The situation is fraught with more dynamite when both the husband and wife have long work histories and the man is forced to retire
before the wife. Now she brings home a paycheck and he does not.
Now she can discuss what is going on at work and he is constantly
reminded that he is a has-been. If questions come up about spending
money for any particular item she may remind him that "after all, I
am earning the money." He may be restless and lonely and view her
rising and leaving every morning with great distress. When the children
come home they sometimes say: "How's your job, Mother? What
happened to that secretary you were telling us about?" And then later

FIGURE 9

Family Authority Patterns by Generation

Authority Pattern	Self-Reported			Observer-Reported		
	Married Child %	Parent %	Grandparent %	Married Child %	Parent %	Grandparent %
Husband-centered	15	12	22	40	24	34
Equalitarian	80	82	69	42	47	28
Wife-centered	5	6	9	18	29	38
Number of families	107	100	94	96	90	74

SOURCE: Reuben Hill, "Decision Making and the Family Life Cycle," in Ethel
Shanas and Gordon Strieb, Social Structure and the Family: Generational
Relations © 1965. Reprinted by permission of Prentice-Hall Inc. Englewood
Cliffs, New Jersey.

to their father: "And what are you doing, Dad?" The mere fact of his wife's working is a daily reminder to the man that he is doing nothing productive. Because he is at home she may expect him to do the household chores, shopping and errands—none of which she ever expected of him when he was working. It would only seem reasonable that he would ease her life by doing these things. But her asking and his doing them reflects a new power structure in which she is dominant. All his anxieties about himself because of retirement may be reinforced in this situation. One man said quite poignantly: "It isn't that I don't want her to have the satisfaction of working. She always got a lot out of it. But now that I'm retired, the empty house and her excitement when she gets home makes me feel three times as empty and useless." It would take a remarkably sensitive woman to cope with these reactions from her husband.

We have some psychological insight into the role shifts which frequently accompany this shift in power. This has been labeled "role reversal."

Neugarten has hypothesized that the devitalization of marriage after retirement may be due to this factor of role reversal which must be regarded as normative after the male and female menopause. In a study utilizing a special TAT-type family projection test, she assayed role attributes in later life. The conclusion of her long analysis of a Kansas City sample was that women became the aggressive and dominant partners and men became more subjective in adjustment and submissive in attitude. Women at this age insist on manipulating the environment and men make inner adjustments of self to their environment. Neugarten does not relate these role changes to marital adjustment, but such role reversals raise significant problems. What trauma is involved for a husband like Henry in coping with the loss of status and his dominant role which have sustained his sense of self-esteem during his lifetime? What major deprivations result to emotional intimacy due to this role reversal? What does the assumption of power do to the ability of the female to continue to play an expressive role? Is it possible that the loss of power by the husband in the marriage has some correlation with the loss of love, which has been seen to reach its lowest point after retirement?

Role reversal coming at the same time as the loss of work and life roles may cause confusion, flight and fighting.

The authors were holding a group seminar and discussing these problems of role reversal when one of the participants said that she would like the group to consider the case of her parents. Her father had been a very active man both in his business and in the community. He was respected both for his commercial and for his political achievements. But he had been a "seven-days-a-week" man and by the time he was sixty he was exhausted. While he was still in fair health he decided to give up his business, his membership on the county political committee and various other community relationships and withdraw to a life of leisure. The participant said that her mother resented this very much. She liked the popularity of her husband because she basked in public recognition. She liked very much the somewhat frenzied activity and the excitement of always being in the forefront of things. Consequently when her husband decided to retire she decided that she would take his place in public life. As she was well known and knew about all aspects of political life she was well qualified to do this. The husband was aghast at this decision. He wanted her to share his leisure. He thought they had contributed enough, so he was very ill-tempered about it. The result was that when she announced her candidacy for a political office he took a trip. She had expected some support from him, but he was in Europe when the campaign was going on. He had not sabotaged her, however. He had let it be known that he thought she was qualified.

His wife won hands down. When he returned she was twice as busy as he had ever been. She was exulting in her newfound power and responding to every request for speeches, committee meeting, or personal appearances. He found himself relegated to a very lonely and isolated position. But that was not all. When he attempted to give her some advice she spurned it. She was now in command. The new sense of achievement and power extended to their home life. She set the stage. If he wished to trail along with her he could do so but otherwise he was free to do what he wished. Their schedule was determined by her life, not his. They had talked about a long trip together, but now she would not even consider it. They had talked about moving from their large home to a retirement cabin on a lake some distance away. She rejected this idea also.

He wandered around lonely and bereft. It happened that his secretary at work, a widow, had retired when he had because after a long work life she felt she did not want to cope with new management and challenges. They chanced one day to meet downtown and, being lonely, he invited her to lunch. At lunch she mentioned a problem she was having with her income tax. He volunteered to help and they went to her home. At her home he became aware of how much he had missed her and how fond he was of her. It was not long before they were planning regular trysts when his wife had to go away for speeches.

Unfortunately the secretary's neighbor was a friend of his wife and in time this neighbor felt it her moral duty to call the wife and tell her what was going on. A scene resulted and he confessed. But he also indicated why this had happened. She had made him feel like a "nothing." She gave no thought to their life together. After a long and bitter evening they decided to get a divorce. The widow was exultant and was willing to compensate him for all the deprivations he had had at the hands of an "unfeeling wife." But he was plagued with memories of his marriage and he eventually tried to reconcile. His wife, now at the apex of her power, took a hard position and humiliated him. He went through with the divorce and married his ex-secretary. The former wife did not do well in later years, lost her position and power, and became an embittered woman. Our participant bore the brunt of her mother's emotions and now asked for help.

So role reversal devitalizes, separates and destroys some marriages. But this is not a universal reaction. Peterson's study indicated that there are many families where decision-making is based on consensus and where there is little or no reversal of authoritarian rules. Likewise almost one third of the grandparent families in the Hill study (28 per cent) were judged by the observer to have equalitarian roles, while another third were husband-dominated.

Still, as Cuber proved, many of these relationships seem only to be suffering from ennui. It is not role reversal that stymies them, it is simple boredom. Having been married for thirty years there is nothing in their intellectual vocabulary or their sexual routine that can stimulate the other. All they have together is memories and these have long ago become jaded. One of our basic problems is to become creatures of growth so that growth excites further growth. When we bore each other we cease to communicate, as Pineo proved. If we don't communicate the silence is nonproductive. In one sense this is an individual problem because if a person is intellectually and emotionally dead he has nothing to share. But the solution may be a revitalization brought by a couple's awareness that they can do together what neither could do alone. They may now revisit their phantasies and rework their visions of leisure time. They may also recapture some of the meaning of their earlier love affair. If loss of work role also brings a shocking realization that human relationships are also terminated, life is threatening indeed. That moment may bring to the surface decade-old resentments and hurts.

Cuber found that there were many older couples who spent their energy repressing hostility for each other. And we all know of marriages in which the couples stay together only on the basis of mutual emotional starvation. The cost in happiness and longevity of such truncated emotional living is indescribable and irreparable. Better that older couples should rage and shout. Then their ulcers would be relieved and their headaches at least forestalled. Without this, of course, the result is marriages which are extraordinarily mediocre in zest and companionship. An honest appraisal of the emotional tone and sharing would help a great deal. We recently had a weekend with twenty couples in such an appraisal situation. It was an encounter which resulted in self-awareness—and self-awareness is essential if change is to come. We would recommend that couples make an emotional inventory of their relationship and then spend a long weekend assessing the steps they need to take if they are to invigorate the relationship.

Included in that inventory must be the emotional history of the couple. Resentment over basic past economic choices, long-smoldering conflicts over children, jealousies about advantages one or the other presumably enjoyed in years past, bitter memories of affairs—all these plague most couples. When there are any such elements in our own histories it is well to ventilate them, air the memories and what they did to us, and thus clear the way for closer rapport built upon the expressed desires and needs of each partner. Sometimes couples can do this for themselves. Many couples are capable of honest communication if they make such a commitment, but sometimes it is wise for them to ask a professional like a psychologist or a marriage counselor to help them explore the reason for their sterile relationship. In many communities groups of older couples are meeting in churches, psychological clinics, marriage counseling centers, and growth centers where they find help. A simple call to a county or state mental hygiene clinic or to a local church will help locate such assistance. Such a ten-minute telephone call may make the difference between a dull or an inspired marriage for the next and last twenty years of life.

Certainly no positive approach is going to be made to help each other with role identity problems, with role reversal, with persistent emotional conflicts or with boredom unless the couple can learn to talk together. To talk honestly about one's feelings releases negative memories and opens the way for new approaches. One of the basic problems of pre-retirement counseling is that the major blocks to the future described in this chapter are never discussed.

The couple are now going to be with each other more often and for longer intervals than ever before in their married life. It is critical that they take steps to clear away the debris of the years so that they can look beyond to new horizons. These new horizons have to do with new patterns of interests and sharing. If the husband and wife have never discussed things, if they have not during their middle years reached out for some vital common interests—they will have a poor platform for their future. But even these obstacles can be overcome providing they learn how really to share their search for mutual meaning in living.

In the search for meaningful living one posits first the awareness that retirement changes the structure, the expectations and the attitudes of the partners to each other. There is now more time and less money on which to plan. This structure of "more time, less money" must be the ground on which couples look for meaning. Let us give some very specific guidelines at this point.

Guidelines for Retirement Living

1. If possible, find some type of post-retirement group in which a number of couples are exploring ways of enriching their lives. This kind of group helped Clara and Henry and can help almost all of those who participate.

2. Join a retirement organization. The National Retired Teachers Association (NRTA), and the American Association of Retired Persons (AARP), are examples. While formally independent, NRTA/AARP have largely parallel purposes, operate in close cooperation, and maintain joint offices at 1909 K Street, N.W., Washington, D.C. 20006. As the names indicate, NRTA is exclusively for retired teachers, while AARP is open to all persons above the age of 55. These organizations are alert to every possibility of meaningful activity for older persons. Typical are their Tax-Aide program, Consumer Desk program, Driver Education program, and their advocacy program—all of which depend upon the volunteer activity of older persons. Their magazines are full of cogent and carefully considered programs for activities.

3. Join a church group of older persons who are exploring ways of serving the community. Such groups as "Head" in the East or "Shepherd Center" in Kansas City have literally changed the whole lifestyles of those who participate in them.

4. Visit a Senior Citizens Center. The activities there may not be for everyone, but many have imaginative and creative programs offering educational, recreational, and service opportunities.

5. Find a counseling center for older adults and then drop in and talk. The Jewish Family Service in West Los Angeles, for example, has such a Walk-in Center that has sympathetically listened to thousands of older retired persons and then helped them to find meaning in their lives. If you do not have such a center in your area, talk with your minister or with a counselor who is known to have an interest in retirement.

6. Investigate the curriculums of any local colleges. One of the great advantages of being retired is the possibility of following up on the curiosity of the past—*i.e.,* investigating the intriguing questions that plagued us during the years we were too busy to find answers to our questions. Retirement does not mean that the mind retires. It can be as active and responsive in our sixties, seventies and even eighties as it was in our twenties and thirties.

7. Hobbies are best seen as opportunities to use our minds and hands in creative ways. We may want to collect stamps or minerals, study history, learn jewelry-making or knitting. It does not matter what we take up. What does matter is that we find in adult education courses or elsewhere expert guidance so that the instruction we get helps to make that hobby rewarding and creative. Couples do not need to do everything together, but it does make life far more interesting if they can be enthusiastic about a common enterprise.

It does not seem necessary to deal separately with those who have experienced an early divorce and have remarried before they were 35 years old. By the time these couples reach 55 or 60 they will already have been married some 20 to 30 years. In most cases the problem of attrition of interests and atrophy of companionship seems to be about the same for them as for those whose first marriage is still intact. They too have had long enough to become habituated and to have lost mutual interstimulation. Much that has been said about our first type applies to them; so that no special analysis is necessary in this case. They may have had long and continued conflicts with previous mates and with their children, but we will reserve a discussion of those problems for a later time. Couples in early second marriages do not generally differ from those we have already discussed. It is true that they have a slightly higher divorce rate than first-married couples, but such divorces come relatively early in their marital careers, so that this is not a necessary item for discussion here. If such a couple have made it to their mid-fifties or sixties we must assume that their early adjustment was good enough to keep them together until the challenge of retirement comes, at which time, of course, they will face the problems already discussed.

Middle-Age Marriages

The second category which we outlined was that of couples who marry in their mid-years—the late forties or fifties. They may be single, divorced or widowed persons. In general, divorced persons are more prone to a second marriage than are widows. They seem to have better chances for remarriage and they marry in greater numbers and sooner than do those who are widowed. Men remarry at a greater rate than women. It has been calculated that the remarriage rate for men past 55 years of age is five times that for women of the same age. Of course, given the disproportion of single men and women at this age, this remarriage rate makes good sense. Harvey Locke made one of the definitive studies of the success of remarriages. He found that the adjustment score of widowed–remarried was as high as that of persons in their first marriage. His study of the remarriage of divorced persons led him to conclude that divorced persons are also fairly good risks for a subsequent marriage. Goode, for example, found that most of his subjects thought their second marriage was much better than their first, but as none of them had been in the second marriage longer than two years the effect of time upon the second marriage was not measurable. Jesse Bernard went beyond arguing about comparison of the success of first and second marriages and made a profile of the type of person who succeeded in a second marriage. She found these persons to be somewhat conventional, belonging to a higher social class, with no hostility toward their first spouse, with acceptance by children of the remarriage and acceptance by parents, and with a favorable attitude of their community toward the new union. Bernard's analysis of successful factors actually indicates a number of prime considerations for those contemplating marriage in the middle years. If the children object strenuously to the remarriage and become a divisive force between the new bride and groom it well be difficult for them to overcome this problem. If the parents of either the groom or the bride look with great disfavor on the new union, this also will create a burden for the couple that is hard to bear.

Below is a case which came to our clinic because of interference with a late marriage. The man was the object of a concerted drive on the part of his ex-wife, his children, and his parents to prevent the marriage:

James Jones had divorced his wife after thirty years of forbearance on his part of her neurotic behavior toward himself and their children. She was obsessed with phobias. She could not entertain, visit friends with him, or go on family outings. He was very conscientious and tried to get her to obtain therapeutic help, but she resisted his every effort. When the children were in their teens he divorced her. She of course spoke to the children of abandonment, of treachery, and immediately began a campaign of coercion and seduction. She poisoned the minds of her children and his parents. He was watched by detectives and he paid the bill. As he had no lady friends then he came out of that relatively "clean."

Much later he began to date and his wife again instituted a watch. More than that, she visited his parents and related every kind of false witness about her deprivation, his children's deprivation, and his immoral behavior. His children drew away from him and his parents often engaged him in consultation about his behavior.

He found an older woman (she had lost her husband through death) who liked him. Their behavior was circumspect and "honorable." Unfortunately his father died and his mother became enormously demanding. He had to call her at least four times a day and visit once a day. But he was able to resist such dependence on her part and work out a reasonable relationship with her. He could not work out the threat she felt in a new marriage, however. His children, in college, felt that a new marriage would threaten their support and they put pressure on him to disrupt the relationship.

He could tolerate and stand these pressures from his wife, his children and his mother, but his prospective bride found all this too much. At this point the two of them came to the clinic to ask for clarification of their situation.

Some husbands and wives who come into a new marriage bear enormous resentment toward their old mate. This may be because they felt rejected by their mate or because they felt emasculated or defeminized by the divorce. In such cases they are apt to contract a new marriage much too quickly, to prove that they are worthy men or women and that they really are lovable. Sometimes, too, they unconsciously generalize their hostility from their first mate to their second, and make the second mate pay for the mistakes of the first. Again, they may have made a false diagnosis about the reasons for the first failure and have determined on a new pathway which has little to do with adjusting to a new and unique human being.

If the remarriage is the result of a shift on the part of either the male or the female away from a boring marriage and if he or she expects that the new partner is going to provide a constant stimulation each may be surprised at how soon the marriage slips into habitualized patterns. If the male marries his secretary or another woman because he has become impotent with his wife he may soon follow the same course with the second wife. Remarriage is no magic answer to individual problems of growing old. A great many men and women have learned this to their great disillusionment.

We mentioned the damage that displaced hostility can cause these late marriages when it is now focused on the second mate. But there are other kinds of memories that can be just as damaging. If one of the partners had a very good marriage and was either widowed or unwillingly divorced, there is every tendency to make those memories explicit. These remarriages can be very "crowded." That is to say, one mate or the other may constantly refer positively or negatively to the former spouse. Thirty years of intimate association is not going to be forgotten easily, but forgotten it must be. If one compares the new mate with the idealized version of a former mate, nothing can help the situation, because the second one cannot compete. If there are constant reminders that George did a job this way or that way, or George helped this way or that, the second wife may soon be living alone with her memories of George. Nor should one forget that there are many instances of remarriages where the former spouse still thinks he is in love with his former wife and he too makes the new home crowded. He will find all kinds of excuses to intrude on his former wife. He will make phone calls. He will send gifts. This makes adjustment to the new relationship very tenuous and uncomfortable. All of those ghosts must be laid aside with firmness and determination for the sake of the new relationship.

We have considered in this chapter the problems that beset marriages which have lasted since an early wedding, together with the problems of second marriages which were contracted soon after an early divorce; and the problems of marriages which come in late middle-age. All of these have their individual problems due to past relationships, but all of them also have hopeful solutions to the problems. In being very specific about the types of marriages that move into old age we have tried to pinpoint specific problems and to give clues toward solutions. But no couple is exactly like any other couple. All case studies are unique. This means that you who are reading this book must ask questions about your own situation and find your own solutions, either by talking as a couple or by seeking the advice of other couples or therapists. What is essential is that all couples be honest in their appraisal of the situation and creative in looking toward their future.

4

Retirement Marriages

The last group of marriages in our typology concerns those who married after 60 years of age. They are a special group. Despite the devaluation by society of romance in the later years, this type of marriage is increasing in number. We have a few studies of these marriages and also some case studies like the following:

Bill Smith and Margaret Haskins were literally carried into the clinic by Margaret's son. He had called to make the appointment, but his call had given no indication of the major problems that appeared during the confrontation among this small group. The son opened the conference by saying: "Mom wants to marry this guy. It is an utterly impossible situation and I brought them here to have you say that to them!" On hearing this the therapist asked the couple if they really wanted to talk and, if they did, if they would like to talk alone with him. They said they needed to talk and they would appreciate some privacy in their discussion, with some dagger looks toward the meddlesome son. The therapist told the son that as this was a matter that really concerned only the man and woman he could wait in the lobby. He was furious but nevertheless he was ushered out.

When the son had been disposed of, the therapist asked the couple if their children were really the problem and they both indicated that they felt they had no other problem except their children, who insisted that it was foolish for them to marry so late in life. After an hour's discussion it was agreed that a family conference would be necessary to

confront the children and to get at the roots of their seemingly irra-
tional opposition.

When the family conference was held, the son accused the man of
trying to avail himself of his mother's money. The mother defended
her future husband and told her son that the man had already made it
clear that no money of hers would be involved in the marriage. She
also told him that if he persisted in thwarting her happiness she would
write a new will. Though somewhat shaken, the son was still suspicious
and belligerent. The other family members were not so avaricious, but
they wondered if this new marriage would disturb their mother's loyalty to the departed mate. That session ended in a truce and a promise
to return for more consultations. After many weeks even the son accepted the remarriage and grudgingly offered to give his mother away
at the wedding.

This case illustrates two of the many difficulties involved in the
remarriage of older persons. Sociologist Walter C. McKain studied
one hundred couples who had remarried when the bride was over
60 years of age and the groom was age 65 or older. Although these
couples were married in 1960, '61, and '62, they were not interviewed
until 1966. This allowed the couples time for adjustment so that the
study would have some stability in its conclusions about late-life
marriage. Due to the careful nature of his research, McKain was able
to isolate those factors which led to success or to failure in these marriages. He called these the "Keys to Successful Retirement Marriages"
and summarized them in six major points. These form the basis of
this chapter, with the addition of some further considerations that
come from our own studies.

Keys to Successful Retirement Marriages

1. *It is essential for a retirement bride and groom to know each
other well if they are to have a successful marriage.*

This proposition is hardly debatable. Virtually all studies make it
emphatically clear that the marriages contracted after a long courtship and engagement are significantly more successful than those that
result from a short "whirlwind" relationship. It takes time to explore
the personality, the temperament, the subtleties, the goals of a person
in order to discover some reasonable basis for compatibility. We are
always delighted by a profound interest on the part of another person.
We like to keep that pleasure, so we magnify those aspects of our-

selves that are pleasing and limit expression of those which might disturb the growing closeness. This tendency is universal and it tends to obscure the real self. Whether at age 16 or 60, we all do a job of selling ourselves. If we think this is the last chance one has in life for intimacy and rewarding closeness, it would be natural to stress the positive. It takes time for us to read any other person, and age makes no difference in this practice. Consequently to know another person requires a long enough time until the other finally reveals himself or herself. Even after a long courtship and marriage individuals sometimes scratch their head and wonder where the stranger they married came from. This is the period after marriage that brings the "surprises." It is often called the "disillusionment period." Its roots are in the human effort to win . . . either a game or a mate. One would suppose that in later life both men and women become more skilled at this game of deception. There is no real antidote for it, however, partially because we all want to be deceived. We want to believe unbelievable things about the one who is falling in love with us. Time helps, premarital counseling helps, but in all relationships there will always be a certain private area of personality that is not known until sometime after the marriage is achieved.

2. *It is important that the marriage be approved of by the children and friends. If they do approve, the chances of success in marriage are maximized.*

We have already discussed the significance of approval of the marriage by the children and indicated what mischief children and friends can do if they disapprove of the marriage. We want to expand on our observations as to some of the motivation behind such objections.

One of the difficulties that appeared in our case study and that was mentioned by McKain is the factor of family disapproval. Sons and daughters sometimes try to intervene to prohibit such unions. This emotional antagonism may be due, as it was in our case history, to purely economic motives. The son is afraid that what his father had left will be dissipated by his mother's new husband. Of course such economic aspects of inheritance can be easily overcome by the preparation of a marital contract in which it is stipulated that the estates of the new husband and the wife remain separate and previous wills are recognized as valid. The part of the estates that is not reserved for the family of either the husband or the wife then goes into a common pool. More and more couples in later years are solving their inheritance problems in this way.

On the other hand another motivation for the children's disapproval of the retirement marriage is often seen in the son or daughter who has an obsession with past relationships. They feel that the surviving parent ought to be "loyal" to the memory of their father or mother by remaining single. They have idealized their dead parent and they somehow feel that remarriage of the survivor is a betrayal of the earlier union. In a good many cases such an emotional attitude stems from guilt on the part of son or daughter. They are covering some real or fancied neglect by undue reverence when it is too late for them to atone elsewise for past errors. So unconsciously they want the remaining mate to do penance for them. In such cases a good therapist is essential if this conflict is to be resolved.

In other cases the problem is that the children simply consider the readjustment of their own emotions involved in welcoming a new member into the family is too difficult. They find it hard to think in terms of a new father or a new mother. In many cases sons and daughters are so hostile to the idea that their interference, nagging and hostility may disrupt either the possibility of remarriage or its serenity if it does occur. We have seen divorced children standing on the threshold of a remarriage for themselves object violently to the remarriage of a widowed parent. It is essential that older persons try to discover the underlying emotional reasons for dissent and not accept the superficial ones advanced in anger or disparagement. If a couple cannot dispel such attitudes, it is necessary that they call upon a skilled counselor to help them work through this problem. It will not go away in the years ahead.

3. *The degree to which elderly persons adjust to retirement and other facets of aging is important in relationship to marriage. If they have adjusted well, their marriage is more apt to be successful.*

One of the most unfortunate pieces of advice given to older and lonely persons is that all they need is a mate and then their problems of adjusting to retirement will be over. We remember one rather pathetic older man who had followed that advice and later came to our clinic. His statement went like this:

My minister told me that it was not good for man to live alone and that if I would find a widow and just get married I would be happy. So I found a widow and I got married and life is hell. I've got all the problems I ever had plus some I never had before. She doesn't want to do the things I enjoy; she is selfish and wants her way; she can't talk about anything, and I tell you, it's lonelier being with someone you can't talk to than being alone. I thought maybe she'd be an answer, but she's only a problem.

This man had thought that if he simply got a wife, any wife, she would solve the retirement problems he had. And that's sheer nonsense. It is like telling a young couple that if they have a baby their problems will disappear.

We cannot load our problems on another human being and expect that person to make our souls right with the world. What happens psychologically is that we expect too much from the other person. We expect her or him to cope for us, and that's unfair. Marriage is a relationship in which we give equally, and to enter into marriage in order to solve personal problems is unrealistic. If we can't cope with the role changes associated with retirement, it is fairly obvious that we can't cope with the role changes involved in a late marriage.

Older persons contemplating a retirement marriage would do well to assess the degree to which the other has made a good adjustment to retirement. Of course, it is pleasant to contemplate rescuing someone from misery, but all too frequently that misery comes to be shared by both.

4. *Success in marriage is related to the disposal of a previously owned home. If a couple decide to live in a house held before the marriage, the chances of success are diminished.*

One of the McKain's findings was that a couple should not live in the house occupied with a former mate. Sometimes there is a reluctance by the new wife to live in a house that was dominated for many years by another woman. Homes of course are places to live, but they also have many living memories. Each room and chair may have its poignant as well as its humorous associations. Another woman, although gone, may still walk the halls and sit at the table. Only a very careful discussion can locate the tender feelings and help to make a decision as to whether the new marriage can thrive in an old habitat. But the economic aspects of life are also important. We must remember that retired couples live on less than half of their previous incomes. It may be that adjusting to memories is easier than a down payment on a new living environment. There is no easy answer to this dilemma; there is only the need to carefully explore the potential difficulties.

We would add to this discussion the importance of the disposal of memories. Memories can be troublesome in more areas than housing. As one grows older a part of the richness of life is the recall of rewarding times in the past. This is important as we tote up the score, but the past should not be sanctified. If there is too much recall about how happy, how tender, how loving, how efficient a homemaker, how excellent a cook was the last mate, the new wife can be overwhelmed with the feeling that she is competing with a ghost. Marital adjustment is hard enough without crowding the new mate by such constant reminders of the perfection of the last one.

It is a major sin in marriage to call the new mate by the name of the other, particularly in moments of tenderness or passion. Most men and women have fears that they may not be able to cope in a marital situation without facing this kind of barbed allusion. The solution lies in recognizing that every human relationship is essentially unique and novel. What happened yesterday is a beautiful part of oneself. It can be a benediction to all our days. The new mate will want to be sensitive about special days when the only honest mood is sadness or a special inner joy. But the focus of most times together has to be on the new person and the new opportunity. And marriage brings together different persons so that the outcome must necessarily be different. This does not make the new marriage either better or worse than the old one, only different. The rewards can be just as stimulating even if they are in a different area or direction. In some ways the new relationship will be better than the old and in other ways it will not. That does not matter. Some couples can pick up old patterns but generally new ones are more stimulating. A man may marry a first wife because she was in many ways like his mother, but he should not marry a second wife because she looks or acts like the first wife. That is marital suicide.

5. *As in all marriages, the availability of sufficient income to underwrite the marriage is important for success.*

There are economic problems associated with a retirement marriage. The Federal Government puts a penalty in terms of real dollars on many of these marriages. As this is written a single man and a single woman can each receive a maximum of $306 a month from Social Security. But if the two get married, their joint income from Social Security is not $612 but rather $459 because the wife's Social Security payment drops by one half. This accounts for the fact that a great many older persons who love each other have decided that the extra $153 is worth enough to live in "sin." They live together without benefit of the state's blessing in terms of a legal document, but they undoubtedly live better and are able to do more together because of their decision. Recently some older couples have found understanding ministers or rabbis who are perceptive enough to fathom the motivation of such persons and who will perform a religious service of marriage for them even though they cannot produce a marriage license. Thus they can feel that they have a religious compact, that they are spiritually joined in the eyes of God if not by the covetous hand of the state! There is a good deal of agitation about this situation among older persons. The necessity to flout the law does not make them happy. As older persons acquire more "senior power" we can expect that pressure upon the Federal Government may well succeed in changing this rather miserable rule.

It is important, also, to consider many other aspects of economic life beyond those of property disposal, housing and social security. In one sense what we choose to buy is a measure of our value structure. If we are willing to give up our time and money for something, it is obviously of high value to us. If a couple contemplating a late marriage work through such a proposed budget, it will reveal these kinds of values. We remember doing this very thing with an elderly couple who were contemplating marriage. The result was such a revelation of conflicting values that there was no marriage. The man was a sophisticated, hedonistic person who allocated a large amount of money for alcohol and trips to Las Vegas. The woman was a conservative, God-fearing woman who regarded all gambling as sin. In his pursuit of her, he had faithfully gone to church with her and played down his need to drink and to gamble. But when it came to agreeing on those things for which their money would be spent he had to reveal his needs. She, for her part, was immovable in her opposition. They soon reached an impasse that was never settled. Later he was fortunate in finding a companion who enjoyed the fruits of the vine as much as he did. The first woman still talks about her escape from marrying someone who was a "sinner."

In another case the conflict that brought the older couple to the clinic had to do with the man's devotion to esoteric health foods. He haunted health food stores and equated his every euphoric feeling with some new food fad. The woman had come from the Midwest and she had a very healthy appetite for steak and potatoes and gravy. By chance, in dicussing a possible sum for food, this difference arose and before the end of the evening it was apparent that if they got married the preparation of every meal would precipitate the battle of the "bulge."

If persons have lived alone for some time they are used to making monetary and other decisions for themselves. When they are married, the other person will expect to have some part in that decision-making. This can be an explosive area unless not only economic goals but methods of making economic decisions are finalized before the marriage begins.

6. *Marital adjustment is related to the personal adjustment of the bride and groom; if either is maladjusted, the marriage has less chance of success. This finding, however, would apply to all marriages at any age.*

This stricture is both too general and too specific. We do not agree that marital adjustment is related to the personal adjustment of the bride and groom in the sense that the greater the maladjustment of either, the greater the chances of failure in the marriage. Marriage is a relationship. If one person tends to be neurotically dependent but marries another person who wishes above all else to be independent and a leaning post, that marriage may have a fair degree of success. We have seen a great many marriages where the success was due to a strong male taking pride in his care of a frail and helpless female. We have also noted marriages where two somewhat hostile persons got married in order to have a target for their hostility. If the hostility is not too profound there may develop a splendid "intimate enemy" relationship in which each is well aware of the contribution of the other in allowing aggression. The question then is not of maladjustment but of the way in which the maladjustments interweave and satisfy. We would prefer to reword this proposition to say that marital adjustment is related to specific ways in which the maladjustment affects the relationship. If there is grossly manifest maladjustment, it will ruin any marriage. But we are all maladjusted in one way or another and some very splendid marriages have come about because the interplay of maladjustments produced an unexpectedly positive outcome. The proposition, then, becomes this: The greater the maladjustment the less chance of adjustment. But we would even say this with caution.

How many times have we all seen a motherly, protective female watching over her bellicose and impulsive mate? She protects him in social situations, calms his excesses and tempers his impulsivity—all the while exulting in her role. She knows that without her help he would destroy himself. Year after year she watches out for him and explains his behavior. This is her life and she loves him for making it possible for her to play such a crucial role.

We remember very well the explanation one older wife gave of her husband's deportment in our group. She said: "You have to excuse Ben. He's always been kind of like that, only now he's more so . . . angry and suspicious and accusing. But underneath he's lovable. He's just getting old and we have to excuse him. He didn't mean anything by tearing into you." In that situation we thanked God for that woman because she entered a retirement marriage knowing full well the anger and suspiciousness she would have to counter. She not only made it possible for her Ben to have a social life but probably kept him from regressing into a definitely paranoid state. Nor did we feel sorry for her, because she was fully aware of her role and deeply enjoyed it. In fact, if she had married someone who gave her no psychological challenge she might well have been miserable herself.

There are some states of emotional well-being that ought to be taken into account in retirement marriages. One of the toughest tests for a late marriage is that involved in coping with an older alcoholic. Many men and women try to drown in alcohol their failure to achieve a balance in retirement. This presents several problems: For a great many couples excessive use of alcohol is an economic disaster. A second problem is the lack of companionship that results from lack of sobriety. A third problem stems from the retreat to alcoholism itself which prohibits any creative solution to problems. One ought never to marry feeling that the marriage will eliminate the problem; it may only accentuate it.

An even more severe problem is depression. A great many older individuals facing the end of life, the lack of meaning in their life, and/or poor health may withdraw and become listless. They may feel that marriage will pull them out of that depression, but, as we said before, marriage cannot solve individual problems. After such a marriage, which may induce a short period of hope, the depressed individual will realize that the marriage cannot help him and this may induce an even greater depression. It is fairly obvious that a person contracting for marriage with a depressed individual should first ask that person to get help in order to cope with the depression. If that is successful, then marriage can follow.

In addition to those six well-taken points that came from the research done by McKain we would add the following to round out his suggestions:

7. *Couples who are entering a post-retirement marriage should make a definite life plan for the years that are ahead of them.*

If a couple are going to make a commitment to each other for the rest of their life, we think it is imperative that they have some very specific idea about what they are going to do together. They can organize this plan by years, stressing what their first year will be like, the second year, etc., or they can organize their plan according to the amount of resources and time they will earmark for various activities. How they organize the plan does not matter so much as their careful assessment of what they are going to do together for the next ten or fifteen years.

We have found this kind of planning invaluable for two reasons. It tests mutuality of interests and it results in a meaningful map of the future. Both of these have great value. Planning of this type can reduce dreams to reality. Some things all of us would like to do fade away when we match them against our energy or our economic resources. Such planning will certainly reduce the likelihood of a "disillusionment period" in which we discover that our expectations were unreal and fanciful.

8. *Couples who are entering a post-retirement marriage should avail themselves of the opportunities for premarital counseling.*

Premarital counseling long ago proved its worth in the marriage or remarriage of younger persons. Our files are thick with letters from those persons who went through a careful assessment of their plans for marriage. What research we have seen indicates that those who ask for help premaritally have a higher degree of success than those who plunge into marriage with no help. No study has been made about counseling with older individuals, but we have no reason to think there would be any significant difference. In fact, our overwhelming impression from our practice in discussing marriage with older couples has been that it is as essential, if not more so, at this age as it was earlier in life. All the areas of concern noted in this chapter can be discussed with an expert. Areas of potential conflict can be explored. Questions can be investigated and at least partially answered.

Where does one find a competent counselor who sympathetically will venture to work on premarital counseling? One answer is that there are a great many priests and rabbis and ministers, who are increasingly becoming aware of older persons' problems and who are in sufficient contact with older persons to be resonant with them. Also, there are a great many marriage counselors with experience in this field. Those marriage counselors who are members of the American Association of Marriage and Family Counselors have earned that membership as the result of training and supervision. Then, too, there are psychiatrists and clinical psychologists in every large city who are beginning to specialize in the particular problems of older persons. These therapists would be helpful. Some social workers are devoting their time exclusively to the family problems of older persons and they can give valuable assistance. One can inquire about these professionals and locate those who have proved valuable to older persons. Last but not least, it is possible in some cases to find groups of older couples who are engaged in studying the potentials and problems of older persons. Such a group would prove valuable even before marriage.

This same study by McKain asked five significant questions regarding these marriages:

1. Did the couple show respect and affection for each other?

2. Did the couple enjoy each other's company?

3. Were there serious complaints about the marriage?

4. Were the husband and wife proud of each other?

5. Was the couple considerate of each other?

There were other clues to the success and happiness of the marriages which helped the investigators decide whether a given late union was successful or not. When all the indicators were evaluated, the result was that seventy-four out of one hundred marriages were judged as successful and "only six of the remaining marriages appeared hopeless." The author of the study cautions the reader to remember that some persons who married in 1960 and 1961 had died and that others refused to be interviewed, so that if these had been available the results might have been somewhat different. It is fair to conclude, however, that this study shows a high rate of success for marriages of older persons.

We would like to conclude this chapter by emphasizing that the McKain study showed a high degree of success of retirement marriages. Our own experience indicates that these marriages can not only be "successful" but also highly rewarding to those who make the venture. But obviously not all are equally rewarding. Our goal in this chapter has been to indicate some of the obstacles to the success of the marriage. These obstacles are not insurmountable, but they do require thought and analysis. We do not like to see any person at any age make the leap into marriage only to become disillusioned. Our goal is to make retirement marriages more promising and fulfilling. This is made possible by what we know about the problems of such late unions. We would be very unhappy, however, if anyone interpreted what we have said as being negative about love in the later years. We are profoundly optimistic about the value of tenderness and closeness in those last years. Our only goal is to maximize them.

5

Sexual Achievement in Marriage in the Later Years

Years ago when the authors were beginning their study of the family in its later years they visited with a psychiatrist and a psychologist who were resident counselors for a retirement community. Without hesitation both practitioners said that a disproportionate number of the presenting problems they dealt with had to do with sexual difficulties. They estimated that there were twice as many sexual problems in this population as all other problems combined. Upon further discussion they also agreed that the presenting sexual problems often masked much more profound problems of human relationships, of individual psychological problems such as depression, and sometimes even physical difficulties. In this chapter we shall not only review in depth the obvious problems of impotence and frigidity but also relate these to the social and personal problems which they represent.

It is easy for a couple to point to the fact that somehow they have lost the sexual joy they experienced in earlier years, but it is much more difficult for them to understand the intricate relationship between their history as a couple and the psychological and health processes which produced these sexual inadequacies. We have spoken before of the self-fulfilling prophecy as it relates to disengagement and withdrawal from society. The same process occurs with sex. Society has long felt that when a woman comes to the menopause, when Nature tells her that her child-bearing years are over, she should also accept the fact that with the atrophy of her ovaries her sexual life, too, is over. Great sexual interest on the part of a young man indicates *machismo* and he is much admired by both men and women. But when an older man shows the same kind of sexual interest he is called a "dirty old man." Older persons are made to feel ashamed of their completely normal sexual response patterns. Thus they are deprived of an activity essential to both their mental and physical well-being. Through these two chapters that deal with sex we must keep in mind the power of the social milieu in defining for all of us how we are to feel about ourselves. Our goal as friends of older persons must be to help them to free themselves from enslaving myths and, incidentally, to free ourselves, because as we become older we too will be subjected to these same destructive myths.

Part of the task in destroying these myths is to establish a realistic appraisal of the sexual potential of older persons. The selfsame myths have prevented us from doing much research along this line. Masters and Johnson remark that it was very difficult for them to get samples of older persons to study. Obviously the myth helps perpetuate itself by thus curtailing our efforts to do research. In spite of such difficulties, however, there has been research on a broad front. And what we say in these chapters on sex in the later years is based on study and not speculation.

Masters and Johnson have done superlative work in objectively assaying sexual potentials for older persons. The chapter in their book *Human Sexual Response* called "Geriatric Sexual Response" is a major breakthrough, even though they indicate that it will take another decade to gain sufficient biological data to speak with the same assurance about oldsters as they do about younger persons. Their study involved 61 females (ages 41 through 78) and 39 males (ages 51 through 89). Those who wish to pursue the biologically related changes in detail should read that chapter. We shall only summarize the conclusions which seem most relevant to the task in hand. Masters and Johnson found that:

1. The vagina loses length, width and vaginal-wall thickness and "a significant degree of involuntary ability to expand under sexual tension."

2. Lubrication due to sexual excitement is delayed, but generally can be produced in one to three minutes.

3. Orgasms develop in identical fashion to younger women, but are of somewhat shorter duration.

4. The intensity of physiologic reaction is diminished.

However, none of these changes inhibit rewarding sexual response because "the aging human female is fully capable of sexual performance at orgasmic response levels." Two very significant further observations were:

1. Adequate endocrine replacement *easily corrects* vaginal burning, pelvic distress, and painful uterine contractions associated with orgasms.

2. In those cases studied where the woman had had regular sexual expression once or twice a week she had maintained sexual capacity.

Both Kinsey and Masters and Johnson suggest that how a woman reacts sexually in the later years may be a matter of her sexual history. Those women who had sexually rewarding marriages move through the menopausal and post-menopausal years with little change in the frequency of or interest in sex. On the other hand if a woman has had an unsatisfactory sexual life she may welcome her advanced years as an excuse to forget sex.

These data indicate that there is no physiologic reason whatsoever that indicates any need to abandon the rewards of sexual intimacy for the woman. Indeed, new discoveries regarding the helpfulness of estrogen and progesteronic replacement may make restitution of tissue decline and thus make sexual intercourse much more satisfactory. The one seemingly important factor here is the continuity of sexual life. When there is a regular sexual life, nature adapts or preserves.

Masters and Johnson made the same kind of comparisons between young men and older men. Some of their more relevant findings are:

1. The older the male, the longer it takes for full penile erection.

2. The penile erection may be maintained in older men for "extended periods of time."

3. The full penile erection once lost, with or without ejaculation, will not return as soon in older men.

4. The number of expulsive contractions associated with orgasm are fewer for the aging male.

5. As with the aging female, the aging male undergoes a reduction in physiological efficiency.

Again the researchers observed that:

1. The maintenance of healthy sexuality for the aging male depends largely on the consistency of his sexual activity.

2. In a high percentage of cases, males over age 50 who have "a secondarily acquired impotency" can be trained out of it and restored to potency.

Masters and Johnson have assembled a group of important factors that relate to the loss of potency. They are:

1. Boredom stemming from the monotony of a repetitious sexual relationship.

2. Preoccupation with economic and occupational goals to the exclusion of communication and sexual energy.

3. Fatigue.

4. Overindulgence in food or alcoholic beverages.

5. Physical or mental deprivations of either the person or the partner.

6. Fear of sexual failure. (The vicious cycle of fear of failure producing failure.)

The male does not go through a climacteric comparable to the menopause. The levels of testosterone go down quite gradually all through the last half of life but never catastrophically. This is also true of sperm production. Again, the most critical items seem to be physical health, psychological mood, and consistency in sexual activity. But even when there has been a period of impotency and lack of activity a proper reconditioning can often restore potency. We shall look at impotency in more detail later.

These summaries of feminine and masculine potentials indicate that the only thing we have to fear is fear itself; that paradoxical though it may seem the more adequate and consistent the sexual life during early and middle ages the more rewarding it will be during old age. "To him that hath shall be given." A well-balanced life giving due concern to economic, family health, recreation and sexual components has the most promise for old age.

One cannot understand the sexual life of oldsters simply from a description of physiological changes that are attendant on aging, just as one cannot understand the sexual life of younger people by discussing hormonal or organ capabilities. Human beings are far more than hormones or sexual organs. They are interacting, related persons hungry for closeness. They need to have shoulders on which to cry and eyes to see their exaltation and respond. They need comfort in distress and laughter for perspective. They covet permanence in relationship so that what is shared today builds into what may be shared tomorrow. Every block to understanding and every stern word that separates will determine the degree of that closeness and may cause withholding in an embrace. Every tender caress and gentle stroke brings that closeness and closes the gap between aloneness and togetherness. To be *with* someone, really *with* is the maximum good of life. And if a preoccupation with job or career or money is given top priority then closeness diminishes. If perfectionism causes constant criticism and insecurity, then sexual response has to be tentative and partial. One supposes that as the years pass human kindness becomes a greater priority and fame and fortune less. It may be true that some career persons, like stage actors, may still put adulation by a public ahead of intimacy but such persons must be few. As we grow older, the values of persons transcend those of achievement. It is here that a great many love and sexual relationships founder, because forty years of neglect are not easily mended.

That neglect is often marked by the absence of verbal and physical stroking. One has to be with another person in body as well as in spirit. A great amount of research has gone on with kittens, baboons and children to prove that some form of skin contact is essential to good health. The desire for contactual relationships is evident for all age groups. Older persons need very much to be stroked, caressed, kissed and hugged. They also need to touch. All of this is encouraged among children and youths, but is often seen as reprehensible in older persons.

What we are saying here is that sex is fundamentally dependent on tenderness. If there has been a vacuum for forty years in terms of

closeness, no Masters and Johnson can repair the separateness by as-
suring us of techniques whereby we can enhance our physical interactions. It is true that monotony may be a bar to good sexual relations in older persons, but only if there was nothing deeply shared
through those years. Sex in a good relationship means sharing appreciation and gratitude; it means respect and concern. To lie together
in contentedness and relaxation with thoughts of thanksgiving for the
day or month past is not monotonous. We need to modify what Masters and Johnson said and to indicate that it is not only monotonous
sex relationships which are involved but also a devitalized and desul-
tory life together that has been devoid of either appreciation or spontaneity. They are accurate in asking that sexual behavior be spontaneous and explorative, but they should also indicate that all life is
holistic and therefore a relationship with no spontaneity cannot produce sexual activities that are spontaneous. Sometimes what is needed
is a complete revitalization or reconstruction of the hour at break-
fast as well as the hour in bed.

We have hinted that disillusionment about sex often follows upon
disillusionment about the other person. Let us be more specific. The
following case history indicates that sexual deprivation was only a
clue to other deprivations:

The story Mary told on entering our office was marked by naiveté and
pathos. She was a 63-year-old woman married for her second time to
Henry R. He had seemed during the late courtship to have a rather ex-
traordinary consideration for her welfare. He wanted to know what she
needed, whom she saw, where she went, and how she spent time when
not with him. They had early developed a close intimacy physically and
both of them were rewarded by a sexual closeness that had eluded them
in their first marriages. They liked good music and good sports, both
participant and observing, so that she had found no reason not to accept
him when he proposed. In fact, she had looked forward to a marriage
that would be superior in both its physical and cultural aspects to her
first marriage.

The honeymoon and early marital adjustment period was "divine."
All her expectations of his attentiveness were fulfilled, and she anticipated nothing but joy the rest of her years, or until they were separated by death. The first intimation of trouble came when he demanded
that she give up her job at which she had worked for over thirty years.
They had discussed her job very carefully before the nuptial agreement
and he had been fully willing that she should work until retirement or
even a year beyond. But three months after the honeymoon he began

to demand that she leave her employment. He gave a great many reasons, to wit: He loved her so much that he could not bear to be away from her for eight hours a day. Their pensions were sufficient so that she really did not have to work. She was too tired after working so that it took away from their enjoyment of each other. None of these rationales appealed to Mary. Somehow they did not ring true and she found herself even more determined to keep working than she had been when she had discussed it premaritally with Henry. Another fact began to enter her consciousness. Somehow every noon Henry managed to be around her work. Sometimes he would unexpectedly drop in just before the noon break and want to take her to lunch. On several occasions she saw him meandering about across the street and she had the distinct impression that he followed her to lunch and back to work again. Being naive she only wondered about this, but one day her boss came in with fire in his eyes and she was to learn more about Henry's surveillance.

Henry had tried to hire a firm to tap the telephone wire of the company who employed her. The surveillance outfit had a foreman who was a friend of Mary's boss and he had promptly called her boss and told him what was going on. Her boss traced it down and found that it was Mary's husband who was behind the tapping effort. He was furious, not at Mary who was a trusted employee but at her husband. He was as kind to Mary as possible, but he let it be known in no uncertain terms that he wanted to know what was going on. Of course Mary didn't know, but she promised to find out.

When Mary got home she mustered her courage and asked Henry what he was doing in trying to tap the phone of her company. Then, in a moment of rare insight, she asked him why he was always around at lunch. Henry became righteously indignant and said he knew Mary was having an affair with her foreman, that everyone knew it, that she was making a fool of him, and he had every right to try to prove her unfaithfulness. She was astonished and vainly protested her innocence. Henry said she could prove it by quitting. To this she would not agree and the look on Henry's face indicated that she had proved to him her unfaithfulness. From then on there was no tenderness and no sex.

Mary did her best from then on to prove how faithful she was. She would hurry home from work. She took a sandwich to lunch and never left the building, but still Henry regarded her with a jaundiced and suspicious eye. She felt hemmed in and one day in desperation talked with her foreman in an effort to learn how she might prove even less blameworthy. But John, her foreman, had long adored Mary. He suggested that the business was no place to discuss this, and that tomorrow they should leave during their coffee break for an hour's discussion at a restaurant or "somewhere." They left at different times and by different

exits and finally wound up at John's apartment where he proved himself
a most sympathetic ally. They laid careful plans to assuage her husband's
suspicions. But this involved much planning and during the planning
Mary came to feel much appreciative of John's concern . . . appreciative enough so that she ended up in John's bed. The end result was a
divorce and a long affair with John.

Mary came to us just after the divorce with great feelings of guilt and
bewilderment that she could have done such things. She never meant to
have an affair. She only knew that she was resentful and bitter about
her husband's lack of trust and her own deprivation in terms of tenderness and sexual response.

We have encountered a great many such persons. They have entered
an early or a later marriage with "great expectations" based mostly on
their own projections and the marriage itself has been entirely disillu-
sioning. The mate has proved that he was only "selling" his best self
before marriage and was concealing very neurotic or even psychotic
tendencies. After the marriage, when he felt secure, these tendencies
bloomed and our Marys found themselves baffled and bitter. One
cannot cope with a paranoidal person ridden with feelings of suspicion
and hate.

There are myriads of ways in which troubled persons project those
inner troubles upon their mates. It is a timeworn psychological method
of coping to project one's own problems upon another person. So the
extremely hostile person makes his mate hostile or the hypochondriacal
person tries to prove that his mate is ill. This not only brings confusion to the mate but it also evokes retribution from the maligned
one. If the ego of the mate is not strong, it will occasion doubt and
sometimes even illness. Then the mate responds with either com-
pliance or attack. The attack is healthy, but it ruins the possibility of
any emotional closeness. From then on the marriage resembles a primitive battleground. No one is quite sure what has happened, but the
early dreams are shattered and the possibility of meeting emotional
and sexual needs is diminished. It is even worse when the mate is dependent and uses courtship as a way to ensure that he or she has someone on whom to lean for the rest of their life. After marriage the
dependence becomes revolting and any real relationship is over. A
great many individuals depend on marriage to furnish objects for their
hostility, their paranoia, or their dependence. These marriages were
made in hell and there is no mutuality or sexuality about them.

But even in more secure marriages the aftermath of middle age coupled with the expectation given by society of eventual sexual failure can result in agony. Let us look at the complex problem of impotence of the man and see how this can occur. Let it be said first that as any man gets older an experience of impotence now and then is normal. His natural store of energy is more easily depleted and any great strain can render him impotent on any given night. This is natural but his alarm about it is not. His alarm or anxiety may trigger such tension that he may fail on his next attempt which will only make him more anxious. This is what we mean by secondary induced impotence and it has more to do with self-image than it has to do with any real physical potential for potency. Most men equate potency with masculinity with self value. *Potency equals masculinity equals worth.* So when he fails even once the man becomes alerted to disaster. Thus his fear may actually produce that event of which he is afraid.

This is tragic because there are sufficient causes for impotence other than a self-induced psychological one. The most common psychological cause is depression. In fact the physician often can diagnose depression simply from a conversation initiated by a man who comes because of his impotence. This is not the place to detail the complexities of depression in aging persons. Depression is the most frequently encountered mental reaction of older persons who face the loss of all the things they value—economic power, relatives and friends, physical agility and self-approval. The great crises of retirement, ill health and death are specters that haunt many aging persons who have not learned to cope with either the expectations or the crises themselves. In a great many cases the depression is so severe that the person loses all mental and physical mobility. He withdraws from stimulation and contact. Small wonder that associated with depression is impotence. He feels impotent about every phase of his life and this feeling is translated into inability to hold his head or his penis high. He shrinks as a person and as a sexual partner. His motivation is gone and his interest is gone. Treatment that would focus on his sexual impotency is bound to fail or have only sporadic success because the impotency is only symptomatic of much more profound psychological and social needs. The psychiatrists are entirely accurate in insisting in such cases that the total person be involved in care, not just the manifestation of his moods in impotency.

The issue is extraordinarily complex because if a man has cherished a good sexual life and his depression results in inability to perform, that fact reinforces and authenticates his depression. He can now think with justification that life is passing him by and the values of the past are gone. He is too old to live and the joys of the past are lost. So his impotency is a kind of final statement by fate that he has a right to his depression and to his withdrawal and his misery. So he becomes more depressed and withdrawn. It is a moving moment when an older patient says: "And even my ability to love is gone . . . there is nothing left." But the aware therapist knows that the impotency is dependent on the depression and that when the patient, through therapy, can arouse new interests, he will also be capable of sexual arousal. To seize on that moment of hope is important in treatment. As a realization of the loss of vitality creates new depths of depression, so signs of virility are building blocks to hope. At this moment there are probably a thousand men reading this book who have given up the possibility of intimacy when that resignation is unrealistic and, in fact, stupid.

Most severe forms of mental distress result in some degree of impotence. Schizophrenics have about half the sexual activity of non-schizophrenics. Much mental distress is the final product of destructive relationships. These relationships need to be reviewed and articulated if a person is to inherit the kind of full life he should have in his older years.

There are physiological factors involved in impotency that are lethal to a good sexual life. One of these is the simple matter of drinking. As one faces the role changes and the crises of age one may take refuge in the soothing half-conscious state of mild or severe alcoholism. The myth that alcohol somehow increases potency is a destructive fairy tale. As a matter of fact, alcohol depresses the nerve centers that are essential to sexual response. Often the therapist who is consulted about sexual problems finds in taking a case history that the individual has effectively destroyed his capacity simply by drinking.

Recently a couple in their seventies called the clinic to ask for an interview. We routinely ask for a statement about life-style that is very specific in terms of food and drink. Early on in the interview it was determined that the husband had four or five stiff drinks every night after dinner. While there were, as there always are, some relationship problems that inhibited the sexual life of this couple, the main query had to do with his drinking pattern. It was explained to them that alcohol is not a stimulant and that the husband's behavior had been self-defeating. Our contract with them was severe. No drinking but much touching and caressing to help overcome the habit. In a short time his impotency disappeared and the husband was quite happy to substitute his sexual rewards for the dubious values of alcoholic oblivion.

The relationship of impotency to some of the major physical decrements associated with aging has been studied. It is generally understood that all disease results in both physical and psychological losses to sexual virility. As early as 1798 the association between diabetes and impotence was noted. During the last twenty years a number of studies have shown that between 30 and 60 per cent of all males with diabetes will lose potency. The causes for this are complex and may lie in the changes in the nervous system or abnormalities of the small blood vessels, or change in hormonal balance. However, often the impotence is due to such related factors as an unfortunate response to such drugs as antidepressants or tranquilizers or to emotional or marital conflict. Dr. Richard D. Amelar, president of the Society for the Scientific Study of Sex, estimates that 90 per cent of impotence problems are of psychological origin. It is important for any person, with or without diabetes, to ascertain whether emotional factors are not more significant than the disease.

In the popular mind there are many questions regarding heart disease and sex. Again the fear associated with possible heart attacks may inhibit effective performance. The hypertensive person certainly is much aware of the possibility that passion may cause mischief. Elliott Howard, a cardiologist in New York City, counsels against "all out" sexual exercise and toward a more restrained type of sexual expression. He outlines a program of conditioning exercise, of drugs to lower systolic pressure immediately before intercourse, elevation of the head of the bed, and a period of rest after sexual contact. It is obvious that such a program has to be conducted under the direction of a cardiologist, but it is hopeful in that such programs have been carefully considered and used.

What happens to sexual function after cardiac surgery? There are some studies, such as those of Kenneth Hart and Donald Korfeld, who studied 800 members of the Mendel Hearts Society as to sexual performance and pleasure at periods of six and twelve months after heart surgery. After twelve months some 49 per cent judged their sexual performance was improved, 43 per cent said it was the same, and 9 per cent said it was worse than it was before surgery. Dr. Stanley Heller, a psychiatrist at Columbia University College of Physicians and Surgeons in New York City, in commenting on these studies says: "Despite the fact that physiological studies demonstrate the fact that intercourse is no more taxing than climbing a flight of stairs at a brisk pace, doctors rarely raise the question of when a patient can resume a sexual life."

A related question has to do with the sexuality potential of men and women who have experienced a good recovery from a coronary attack. Two cardiologists, Hellerstein and Friedman, have analyzed this problem in some detail. They have developed a "sexercise tolerance test" which enables them to make quite specific recommendations regarding intercourse after a coronary. Their study has to do with the ability of the person to perform certain exercises like vigorous walking on an up-and-down two-step test, or to attain a certain level on bicycle riding without symptoms. All these recommendations are based on study, but each person is an individual, of course, and ought to find a cardiac doctor who will work with him or her on the problem. It should be noted that women are not regarded as having as much risk during postcoronary sex as are men, but they too ought to follow the specific directions of their doctor. The best general answer seems to be that given high blood pressure, cardiac surgery or a coronary, a modified sexual life is still possible under the direction of a doctor.

The problem for the woman in our society is distinctively different from that of a man. The years after menopause are for some females years of liberation from the fear of pregnancy and the oppressive care of children and adolescents. Quite frequently the later years of a woman's life are much freer from the kinds of fears that often dominate a male and result in his struggles with depression and impotency. For the woman there is often a "surge of sexuality" that speaks of freedom from fear and new energy potentials. Kinsey told us that the woman's libido after the menopause remains at what it was or sometimes even is slightly higher. Her psychogenic freedom may result in far more openness to sexual adventure. There is no physiological reason why she may not have rewarding sexual experiences as long as she lives, but there may be social reasons.

Susan Sontag wrote an incisive article for the *Saturday Review of the Society* in which she postulated that "the social convention that aging enhances a man but progressively destroys a woman" becomes an instrument of oppression. Her thesis, simply put, is that the "Double Standard of Aging" means that women become "sexually ineligible" earlier than men do. So, for women, aging "means a humiliating process of gradual dequalification." A woman has greater handicaps than men simply because of the calendar. An older man may marry a much youger woman, but the reverse causes ridicule.

We pointed out that impotence is often the result of the male's profound anxiety about aging. In a somewhat different sense a woman's view of her sexual self is determined by the social judgment that she is no longer young or beautiful or desirable. "Every birthday sounds a new defeat." Her self-view is a reflection of our emphasis on beauty, on youth, and on the value of women as persons. Because society has never let women be completely adult they are considered obsolete much earlier than men.

Sontag thinks that men view aging with apprehension, but that women view it with shame. All of the vast industry to dress and adorn and cosmetize women is the result of "relentless pressure to maintain appearance." This follows because age penalizes women more than men. Women try to maintain the ideal of their youth . . . a smooth skin without blemishes, a slim body with not too much musculature and "feminine" (*i.e.,* graceful) movements. These qualities change with age and so the massive battle waged through cosmetics and surgery never to change. So, says Sontag, "women's sexual validity depends on how well they stand off these natural changes." By social standards, then, an older woman is "sexually repulsive" while a man who may have the identical decrements is not. This is the double standard.

The result of all this is that men tend to choose younger women when seeking a late marriage partner or having an affair. The double standard of aging "sets women up as property, as objects whose value depreciates rapidly with the march of the calendar." So the new Women's Movement is demanding that women be allowed to act their age and not lie about it; to be as competent as they can be, as wise as life has taught them to be; as strong and ambitious as they need to be. Instead, then, of moving from a stage of being worshipped in the teens to humiliating rejection in the middle years and then "obscenely into old women, they ought to become women much earlier and enjoy a long, erotic career, for nature gave them possibility."

This is an important statement by Sontag, but it does not specify what the double standard does to marriage or to a long-established sexual relationship. We suppose that if she had finished her argument she would have said that a woman who has defined her value only as that of beauty and who judges her value by this standard would undermine the possibility of a "long, erotic life." She would do this by the falsity of the image, by the emphasis on the wrong aspects of herself, and her inability to develop into a real and interesting person who would be cherished by a mate regardless of her wrinkles. Thus, her face might be wrinkled but her mind would be young and her capacity to interact with her husband during his growth would ensure more and more depth to the relationship. We suppose that for many a woman it is her tunnel vision or inability to see herself as other than a sexual object, that eventually causes her sexual partner to withdraw. Indeed we had a recent case which nicely delineates this situation:

Billy Joe had only one passion; it was to maintain her perfect face and figure. All of her energy and dollars were spent in this endeavor. For years her husband, Gene, felt that he was enhanced by the jewel he had on his arm. But as the years passed he often found that his friends were kind to Billy Joe, but never wanted to spend much time with her. Her vocabulary consisted of cosmetics and reducing regimens. She rarely looked at the newspaper or read a magazine. Books were never opened. As Gene moved into his fifties he began to be given important community responsibilities. His outlook broadened and he became involved in working for retarded children and later the Community Chest. But all this bored Billy Joe. She had a face and figure to exhibit and she disliked serious people who had no time to admire her. One night Gene reviewed what had happened to them and concluded that he had raised a hothouse plant that could only thrive under bright lights and with much liquid, and he did not like what he saw. They talked about it and she told him that she thought every effort she made was to stay attractive to him. He told her that attractiveness is more than facial tissue. She was shocked because her lifelong anxiety had been to remain "young and feminine" so that Gene would not ever be tempted by another woman. She had a horror of aging because aging meant rejection. He had a horror of this child-bride who in her fifties was still childlike. He was so turned off that sex was no longer enough and he left her.

The absurdity in this situation is that, as a young man, Gene wanted precisely what he got and his male friends wanted the same thing. Billy Joe did not adopt her life-style in a vacuum. She was listening to the voices of both her male and female friends. They all helped focus her in one direction. She had only one child and she did not nurse that baby for fear nursing would ruin her contours! Furthermore, during their early marriage Gene reinforced that notion. She remembers that he once wistfully told her to "stay just as young as you are."

This philosophy has a good deal to do with that inner radiance which comes from good health. Women feel that muscles are ugly. They allow their natural-born strength to dissipate through disuse. Even now it is surprising, with what we have learned about exercise and its contribution to good health and zest, that the movement to stay fit is practiced generally by men. This may be one reason for the fact that although nature has decreed that women should live longer than men, they also have far more illnesses than men. Some sexual dissatisfaction that stems from unsatisfactory sexual response on the part of the wife can often be traced to her physical indolence. Many women are so set on keeping a trim figure that they have little energy to invest in sex. There is no response or little response from them in the sexual embrace. The entire sexual apparatus is muscular, and if muscles atrophy they cannot function. Years ago a physician developed a way through a series of exercises to control incontinence which was due to the weakening of the pubococcygeus muscle. He was at first surprised to have women report that for the first time in their lives they were having satisfactory orgasmic responses. It may be that society has decreed that women should be "fragile" if they are to be attractive, but fragility is a splendid ground for poor sexual performance.

A still further and more profound implication of Sontag's thesis has to do with psychological derivatives from this definition. If it is indeed true that many women are culturally aware that their whole worth rests on facial beauty and they are also aware that aging is inevitable, the degree of profound hostility engendered by that insoluble problem would tend to militate against any closeness. Children would be resented because of the physical toll they took and husbands would be an object of hatred because there could be no security in the relationship with them. Sexual intimacy would be to some extent grudging and partial. One would expect that in many cases aging itself would reveal much bitterness which had been hidden before that time. Indeed the description of some older women as witches might stem from that process. Sontag uses that term in another context. Perhaps the phenomenon of role reversal mentioned in a previous chapter can be partially explained by the irony of woman's place in such a system.

Indeed, some of the already complex descriptions of frigidity might profit from introducing this consideration. Women are frigid because of social definitions that sexual enjoyment is immoral for women. Let us add that some women are frigid because of the anxiety induced by an impossible double bind. Also, older women are frigid sometimes because they have had awkward and insensitive sexual partners. They have often spent miserable nights because their husbands had no understanding of their sexual needs and left them unfulfilled and frustrated. If this goes on for years it is not surprising that some women welcome menopause as a plausible excuse to end the whole unrewarding business.

It is true as we stated in describing the physical changes in women that some may suffer pain because of lack of lubrication or cramps, but these conditions are easily relieved by the use of a harmless lubricant or by estrogen-progesterone replacement. We think that most frigidity in older women is the result of their sexual history or their fears of aging. Seldom does it have much to do with a physical decrement. Still, we send our older clients who come to us with sexual problems for a thorough gynecological evaluation because there are a number of conditions which may need the attention of a physician.

There are some general cautions about sexual interaction that need some emphasis. In our counseling with younger persons we always emphasize the fact that sexual energy ebbs and flows depending on other investments. As we grow older, selecting an appropriate time for sexual intercourse is even more important. It is, of course, far better to have one rewarding experience than three that are haphazard or frustrating. One factor that is generally important for all ages is cleanliness. Nothing turns off a mate so much as disorder, whether personal or in a room. Body odors, bad breath, stringy hair, and so on, are not erotically pleasing. One loves to caress a clean body and smooth hair. Timing is important, too. A sexual partner likes high priority. The man who says to his wife time after time: "I'll come to bed after this TV show, dear; wait for me," doesn't endear himself. She will probably be sleeping, or feigning sleep when he comes to bed. We are always amazed at the inconsiderateness of some persons. They may note that their mate is deep in some project or book and still demand that their needs be met that instant. The mate may conform to the request, but consideration is a better basis for good response. Thoughtlessness in any of these matters can diminish sexual response.

Our focus so far in this chapter has been on individual problems as they relate to sexual effectiveness in the later years in a marriage. But probably the most significant aspect of healthy physical interaction is the relationship itself. Couples tend through the years to develop rituals that grow to have less and less meaning. They greet each other and say good night in the most casual and meaningless ways. What they generally are saying by such rituals is that they have nothing to say that is new or exciting. The good-morning and evening kisses are perfunctory and their greetings to each other are pallid. Over the years their roles may have separated and their interests become diverse. The same habituation may account for a meaningless sexual life. They may have drifted into a set habit in which he approaches her in the same way he has for thirty years. She describing this, says: "It's no new thing." She may phantasize another man to give some excitement to the event or she may simply contemplate her grocery list for the next day. Of all the complaints that are registered with a therapist this seems to be Number One: There is nothing new or exciting. Sex has become routine and boring. His tendency or her tendency is to say: "Oh, *that* again." The counter to this routine is new exploration of sexual techniques, new ways of demonstrating affection, concern for the reaction of the other.

Of course that means going the "extra mile." It means discussion of the other's wishes in terms of sexual arousal and desired form of intercourse. This may be more difficult for the female than the male. With her anxiety and conditioning she may find it trying to meet her husband's need for new stimulation. Everyone in her past has told her to be submissive and modest. But there is one controlling factor that she ought to realize. As a male becomes older it is more difficult for him to achieve complete penile erection. He can achieve this as long as he lives, but the cooperation of his partner is essential. Routine approaches no longer satisfy or stimulate. She may have to finally abandon her pose of modesty and her assumption of submission, because now he needs stimulation. When they were young all he had to do was hold her and he was ready for bed. Now, much to his chagrin, he may have the thought but the action is more difficult. Difficult, yes, but not impossible at all! If she knows these needs and loves him, to move toward meeting those needs is not asking the impossible. But she has different needs, too. We stated that lubrication comes later than previously. She needs more fondling and tenderness than before. In one sense nature has provided the ideal mixture; he is slower to arouse and she takes longer to become tumescent. Only routine and lack of imagination can stymie this fit between the two. If he becomes too frustrated with his change and she reacts negatively, disaster may follow. But if they can regard their sexual interaction as changing but still rewarding and discuss openly their individual needs there is no problem of adjustment, and a promise of great fulfillment. We sup-

pose that sexual fulfillment in the later years is far more significant
and reassuring than in the twenties. It carries more freight in the later
years. It is more essential to mental and emotional health. Furthermore, with retirement and the loss of other roles the sexual role may
displace other satisfactions. We have suggested making an extra effort. This means that sexual adjustment after the age of 60 often requires more patience and intelligence than it did when the couple
were in their thirties. It requires consideration of the fatigue factor,
of the frustrations, of the expectations of the other. When a wife in
her twenties says: "I'm too tired" it often means, "You disappointed
me and I will have nothing to do with you." In her sixties it is often
just tiredness and fatigue. Assurances of concern with positive responses to the state of well-being of the other heals the breach and as-
sures later response.

We return to the significance of *tenderness* and *touching* in the later
years. One couple who are in their eighties have told us very frankly
about their sexual selves. The wife said:

"The one thing that has kept us very close together is our willingness
to understand the other. When he needs affection and I'm dead-tired
I tell him that, but then I put my arms around him and stroke his
head. After a while he goes to sleep, but in the morning he's cuddling
me and smiling when we wake up. We have found that it isn't just
sex that is good, it's that touching and closeness." Yet tenderness is
destroyed by routine, by the habitualized and dull routines of the
past. It is also destroyed by what we call the "evil" of history. So many
individuals look backward instead of living in the present that they
cannot react to opportunities of the day. They are the "injustice col-
lectors" who seem to delight in every negative happening of twenty
years ago. This is really emphasizing the dead end of life because yesterday can never be recaptured but today can move forward. There is
no sense in the compilation of hurts because this only traumatizes the
present. Some couples get in the habit of weekly assessing who was
most blameworthy in the years past. This is an exciting way to pro-
mote hostility and frustration. It has no end. What it effectively does
is to close the door to new adventures of the couple and to movement together.

The counter to the exercise of mutual "injustice collecting" is two-
fold: first, a recognition of its futility, and, second, the exercise of
forgiveness. What we did yesterday is irretrievable. Whatever the
motivations or justifications they are in the past and the actions are in

the past. No one can ever change them. But we can forgive, so that the slate is cleaned of recrimination and blame. Then we can venture together to something better than spreading venom. A vignette of such a case is instructive. We listened just last week to a couple indulging in recriminations. Said she: "He just climbed on. Whenever I wanted to be hugged, he thought it an invitation for sex—and sex it was. He never thought of my real need for affection . . ." (and on and on for forty minutes).

And he said: "That may be true, but she so seldom was affectionate that I was always starved. Can you blame me that I took advantage when she was tender?"

In a sense many older couples who have lived together for forty years duplicate their experience. The past is all too vivid in their consciousness and recall. We say to all couples who may be in this bind that every hour of this day is a new hour; every contact is novel; every tomorrow is capable of innovation in relationship. As the years pass, the number of tomorrows grow fewer and we need to invest every moment with joy and sharing. Human beings are the only living things that can transcend the past and structure the future in new ways. A tree when bent is bent for life, but human beings can straighten their trunks and look up at the stars instead of looking back at their misfortunes.

If sex is dull and routine it does not have to remain that way. The extra effort of inserting some gladness in expression and some feeling into touch pays off in increasing closeness and response. Hundreds of our older clients have discovered that they can live abundantly with each other. It is a great discovery.

6

Sexual Achievement for the Single Person in the Later Years

Every male and female needs relationships that are characterized by intimacy, closeness and response as well as by physical touching. The ironic aspect is that there have been no answers for most single persons. The problem is compounded for the person over the age of 55 by the radical disproportion between single men and women. We pointed out that there are four times as many single women over age 55 as there are men. Even if all the single men married women over age 55, that would still leave 7,000,000 single women. Therefore this chapter could well be titled "Sex and the Single Older Woman."

Of course it is possible to argue that at the age of these men and women they ought to be content to live without love or heterosexual contacts. Society has little sympathy for senior sex and even less for the single senior. The increased sexual freedom allowed adults in recent years is not extended to the elderly adult. Our customs, laws and religious norms seem to make the ascetic life the only real alternative for most single older men and women. We wonder whether this is healthy from a psychological or societal point of view. It does seem to penalize a great many healthy and potentially responsive persons through no fault of their own. We want to explore the potentials for intimacy, whether sexual or nonsexual, that are possible in our society. Some of these solutions will not be acceptable to many who read this book or to the counselors who guide them. Yet without such alternatives society is left with an enormous problem and we think it better to look at the values and the problems of the alternatives rather than let individuals simply flounder and grow bitter. Before turning to these alternatives, it is important to identify some of the personal and social conditions unique to the single older adult and others common to all single adults.

Our society is a marrying society, a couple-oriented society. This is true no less for the older adults than for younger adults. Less than 7 per cent of the adult population never marry. Many adults will marry three or four times. One woman who recently married for the third time commented to us: "If anyone had told me at seventeen that I would be married three times before I was fifty-five, I would have told that person that he had rocks in his head—that only movie stars and the jet-setters do that." But those over the age of 65 are the adults doing just that. A recent issue of *Aging* (published by the U.S. Department of Health, Education, and Welfare) carried the announcement of the marriage of Webster Boyd, age 69, to Selma Kelly, age 67, and included the information that it was the fourth marriage for Mr. Boyd and the third for the new Mrs. Boyd. A major difference, then, between the older and younger single adult is that the older adult has most likely been married for 10 to 40 years—that is, most of his or her adult life—and to have been married two or more times.

Our society rewards the younger person and penalizes the older person who marries. Income-tax deductions for married adults make an economic reward for single young adults who get married. But not so for those singles over the age of 65. The *source* of income makes the major difference. In place of salaries and wages, most older adults receive social security benefits and pensions. Tax laws do provide some benefits for older people, but there are hidden penalties. Social security income is not taxable, but if two recipients marry, their combined social security income is reduced, as has been pointed out, by about $150 a couple. Most private pensions include a clause that cancels the payments if the widow of the worker remarries. Thus, a woman with single social security payments and a widow's pension loses the major portion of her income and reduces the potential couple's source of support. Pension reforms and Women's Lib will eventually bring some relief to the singles. But that is in the future. Older adults need to use their influence and political pressure to bring these changes about as rapidly as possible.

An example of this problem is the case of the two residents of a nursing home who fell in love and wanted to marry. As singles, they were able to pay their expenses in the home, but as a married couple they would not be able to afford to stay in the home. They believed in marriage and took the penalty. At last report, the nursing home administrators were trying to raise additional funds to support the couple, who took up no more space after marriage, and required even less attention. Many would say that the couple had no business getting married in the first place. We disagree. We ask: Should adults in the last part of life be denied the comfort and companionship of marriage? Love is necessary for life at any age.

Another difference between younger and older single adults is that most of the older single adults will be women and they are less likely to remarry than single men. Women who were a part of the increase in middle-age divorce statistics are less likely to remarry than are their ex-husbands. Most older divorced men remarry and usually to much younger women. Recent U.S. Census bulletins report that most older men are married and most older women are widowed. Almost two fifths of the older married men have wives under 65 years of age. Statistics on remarriage are not complete, but the states that participated in reporting marriages for the over-65 age group report that less than 10 per cent of the marriages were first marriages for the brides or grooms. Figure 10 shows that in 1972 only 15.7 per cent of older men were widowed, but that 52.8 per cent of the women fell into that category.

As singles, our nursing-home couple spoken of above would have been better off financially if they had forgotten the ceremony. Making it legal cost the couple $102.60 a month in social security payments. Under government regulations their combined social security payments received dropped from $412 a month to $309.40 a month. That is $52.60 less than the amount normally required for their care, by U.S. Bureau of Labor statistic standards. Social Security officials report that the elderly who marry can expect to lose $70 to $200 a month in social security and supplemental payments.

Susan Sontag's double standard of aging is experienced again at the time of the loss of the marital roles. The female gains her identity and self-esteem from the marital roles and therefore experiences more loss at widowhood than does the male when he is widowed. Since most older women gave up early career ambitions *or* never worked, they never achieved a worker role identity. Lynn Caine, writing about

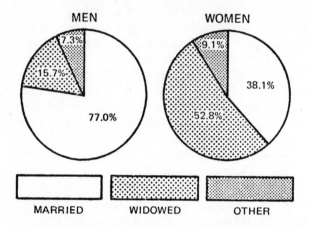

FIGURE 10

Distribution of Older Persons
by Marital Status, 1972

MEN   WOMEN

7.3%

15.7%

77.0%

9.1%

38.1%

52.8%

MARRIED   WIDOWED   OTHER

SOURCE: New Facts About Older Americans, U.S. Dept. of Health, Education, and Welfare, June, 1973

her experience and feelings as a widow, observes: "Our society is set up so that most women lose their identities when their husbands die . . . we draw our identities from our husbands. We add ourselves to our men, pour ourselves into them and their lives. We exist in their reflection and then . . . ? If they die . . . what is left?" Furthermore, she continues: "Death parts women from their loves more often and earlier than it does men. The Darby and Joan ideal, that blissful growing old together, is rare, rarer, rarest. For women, that is."

Kinsey found that age does not affect the frequency of sexual activity for the male and female, but, in contrast to men, single and post-marital females had rates of sexual activity which rank below those of their married peers. The more recent Duke studies show that the marital status of men has little or no effect on sexual activity and interest. In women, marital status has considerable effect on sexual activity, but *little effect on interest.* Unmarried women (widows) in the Duke studies report a decrease in the incidence of coitus from 37 per cent at age 50 to 0 at age 65. However, 25 per cent of them report masturbatory activities at age 70. The opportunity for heterosexual activity on the part of the aging female, unlike that of the aging male or young female, is still more apt to be determined by the availability of a husband and his sexual capacity. Unmarried older men maintain sexual activity and interest at levels roughly similar to married men. Women do not, because there are no socially available partners.

These scientific studies confirm the popular notion that the single older female has a more difficult time in sexual achievement than does the male—and more for cultural and social reasons than for lack of interest or for any inability to engage in sexual activity. These studies explode the myth that menopause for women blunts or ends human sexual capacity, performance and drive. The single older female's decline in sexual activity is related to lack of structured access to appropriate sex partners. Since longevity is unequal for the sexes, and younger men sex partners are socially disapproved of, most women will spend a major portion of their old age as singles without available sex partners.

Although it is more difficult for the older female to achieve sexual fulfillment, there are some single older males who are attempting to find the same fulfillment and who encounter the same "ageism" and economic discrimination that makes their search difficult.

For over twenty years sociologists and gerontologists have been trying to destroy the myth of sexless old age—and with some success. There is general acceptance and approval of older couples' marrying, which is our society's major solution for the problems of sexual satisfaction. However, this solution leaves the majority of older people without socially structured and approved means of achieving sexual fulfillment. Indeed, the senior single is regarded as deviant when he or she overtly expresses sexual interest and needs outside of marriage. The role left for the single older person is most frequently a sexless one.

It is with these social facts before us that we explore the alternatives available for sexual achievement for the single person in the later years. Sociologist Jessie Bernard concluded from her review of research on changing family life-styles that the old life-long monogamous commitment represented by traditional marriage seems no longer to have the monopoly as a design for living. She classified the non-family and neo-family forms of alternatives to marriage into five types or models: The two non-family types are the swinging model and the cocktail lounge model. The three neo-family types are the Berkeley, campus, or companionship, model; the hippie model, and the one-sex community model. It is evident from the titles that these types reflect the sexual freedom which emerged in the Sixties among youth and young adults.

As we adapt these models of alternatives for senior singles, another similarity between the single young adult and the single older adult becomes apparent. Like the young adult the senior single is in a period of life which is more conducive to forming a variety of relationships with persons of about the same age. Furthermore, the patterns identified among the youth were already forms of adaptation to being single practiced by older persons. The difference lies in society's disapproval of these same relationships or styles when practiced by the elderly.

In addition to Bernard's models, we are also including the traditional alternative: courtship and marriage. These alternatives, however, are not mutually exclusive—that is, a person may try *more* than one of them. Nor have we exhausted all the possible combinations of relationships.

Courtship and Marriage

The first alternative is that as many of our older single men and women as possible solve their economic and social-psychological problems and marry. That was our concern in the earlier discussion of retirement marriages. This alternative is the one pursued by those actively seeking a new and permanent partner. Courtship rules for older adults may need to be different, but certainly no stricter than for younger adults. The middle-aged children of the single older people frequently disapprove of their elders' courting behavior. Letters to "Dear Abby" about older parents' courtship behavior have increased. A typical case is one reported recently by a middle-aged daughter of one of the participants.

DEAR ABBY: My mother is 59. Six months ago, Dad died after a short illness and she was so despondent she said she didn't want to go on living.

Well, somehow she got the strength to live because suddenly she tells us that she met a man and he asked her to go to Hawaii with him! I should have said something, but I was glad she wasn't despondent anymore. She said this man asked to marry her, but she refused because she didn't know him well enough. Can you beat that!

The whole family is divided over this. I disapprove, but haven't the courage to say so. I think she's setting a bad example for the younger people in the family. My brother tells me not to be such a prude. He says we should thank the good Lord she isn't crying all over us and wanting to move in.

How do you feel about it, Abby? Does age make any difference? I wouldn't want my 23-year-old daughter going to Hawaii with a man and no wedding ring. Why should I feel any different about my mother?

CONFUSED

Abby's reply was delightful:

DEAR CONFUSED: Every adult has the right to pursue his (or her) own life-style. You may disapprove if you wish, but you haven't the right to impose your values on either your adult daughter or your mother.

One of the major difficulties facing the singles who are seeking new partners is how to meet an eligible older person. Most of our social organizations for singles seem to be aimed at the young and middle-aged singles. The "singles clubs," Parents Without Partners, and so on, are planned for younger persons. The couple we spoke of earlier, Mr. and Mrs. Webster Boyd, met at a Senior Citizen Center cafeteria where the bride was the director. This case, along with the many others which have been brought to us, suggests that as single seniors involve themselves in meaningful community activities they will increase their total life satisfaction and the possibility of finding a new partner.

To facilitate senior marriages we suggest the need for many more trained experts who can do premarital counseling for older persons and their adult children; i.e., counselors who are trained to understand their peculiar problems and speak to them. We think churches and synagogues ought to be manned by skilled ministers and rabbis who can give fundamental guidance. Theological seminaries need to include the counseling of older couples in their training of ministers. In fact, a theology of aging in which religious beliefs are interpreted and applied to all the unique experiences and social situations of the aged needs to become a part of the seminary curriculum.

We would like to influence social policy to be more supportive of the marriage of older persons. To this end, we think the Federal Government needs to look at what its Social Security regulations and pensions are doing in making many older men and women live together covertly. In the absence of such reforms, many older couples solve this problem by having religious marriage services, but without the legal certificate.

Washington State University gerontologists report the case of a 79-year-old single female who is still pursuing an active sex life:

Mrs. S. was widowed at the age of 56. She is tall, thin, and has a healthy glow about her. Her married sex life had been active and satisfying. In the twenty-three years since her husband's death, she reports thirty-five adventures, some lasting the smaller part of an evening, and others going on for as long as fifteen years. Her youngest mate was only 15 years old, while the eldest was 82. Mrs. S. is an intelligent professional woman who spent her professional life in newspaper work, advertising, and public relations. She is the proud mother of loving and successful children.

Alternatives to the Traditional Family

The Swinging Model. Bernard used this term to refer to the well-paid among the unrelated single young adults living in apartments rather than in group quarters. These young people reflect the tendency to leave the parental home early and to find their own design for living with those belonging to their own generation. When the real-estate industry discovered them, it designed luxury apartments for their pleasure with provisions for all kinds of social activities and entertainment.

Applied to older adults, this model refers to those unrelated seniors on fixed incomes who live in households apart from their younger adult family members—that is, not in group quarters—and find their design for living with those of their own generation—the subculture of the retired. Government, nonprofit organizations and the real-estate industry all identified the unique economic and physical needs of these elderly and designed high-rise apartment complexes and retirement communities in which housing and residential clusters make it possible for more male and female contacts. They also included provisions for a variety of social and recreational activities geared to the interests and physical abilities of those in their later years.

The name assigned to this model may be misleading. It does not refer simply to extremely permissive or profligate sexual relationships. It does refer to the desire and need for single men and women regardless of their age to have meaningful relationships of all kinds with their peers. One of the many advantages of retirement communities and apartments is the promise to the female of many male associations in clubs, sports, recreation, church and volunteer work. Since women may be expected to outnumber men in these communities, there remains the assurance of some heterosexual contacts and more opportunities for intimacy apart from marriage.

Older adults, no less than the younger adults, are likely to experience premarital or postmarital sex. Major research on adult sexual behavior supports this view. Sociologist Morton Hunt conducted a comprehensive survey of sex in America in the early 1970's (see Figure 11). He found a surprising degree of tolerance of premarital sex in the general population, even when there was little or no emotional relationship between the partners. In every age group, however, the stronger the emotional commitment between partners, the larger was the percentage of those who approved. Hunt concluded that today's adults are becoming more accepting of premarital sex without affection, but not even the young prefer it; their guiding attitude is "permissiveness with affection." This form, not recreational sex, has replaced the traditional practice of premarital chastity.

Kinsey's earlier studies included women who would be over 60 years of age in the 1970's and who, as we have seen, are statistically most likely to be single. His studies reinforce Hunt's findings (see Figure 12). While there is a steady increase in premarital sex coitus among the younger age groups, we remind the reader that we are discussing the values of older persons. Fewer of that age group, either men or women, have had premarital sexual experience, and those who did experience sex before marriage tended to limit that experience to the person they later married. Moreover, when Hunt sought to extend Kinsey's data, he found an increase in this type of behavior in women born after 1938.

These studies tell us that senior singles seem to have a sex ethic similar to all other adults; that they have been a part of the growing sexual freedom; that they, too, view sex in a liberal romantic way and approve of permissiveness with affection. They lead us to deal realistically with the sex tensions that are a part of being human at any age. Their tensions may take different *forms* at different ages and in different socio-personal situations, but they remain a part of life.

Since all adults have shared in sexual liberation we can expect the adaptation that single older persons make will reflect this change in traditional attitudes toward the sexual behavior of single adults. Given years of adult experience, the single senior would be free of many of the worries and tensions that surround premarital sex experience among young people. Older adults have a different set of worries and tensions related to their adult children and grandchildren. For example, the following case indicates the dilemma of the older single person.

FIGURE 11

Percent Ever Had Premarital Coitus
(total married sample)

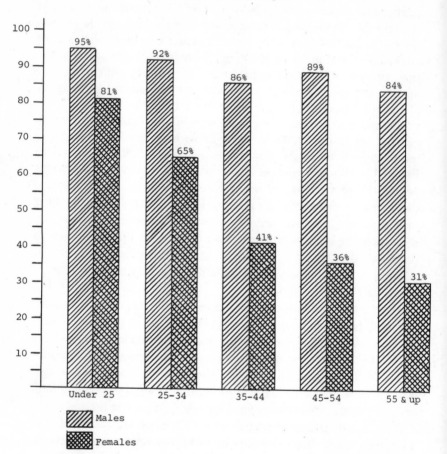

SOURCE: *Sexual Behavior in the 1970's* by Morton Hunt. Originally
appeared in *Playboy* Magazine; copyright © 1973 by Morton Hunt.
Reprinted by permission.

FIGURE 12

Percent of Premarital Coital Partners of Married Females
(Kinsey and Hunt compared)

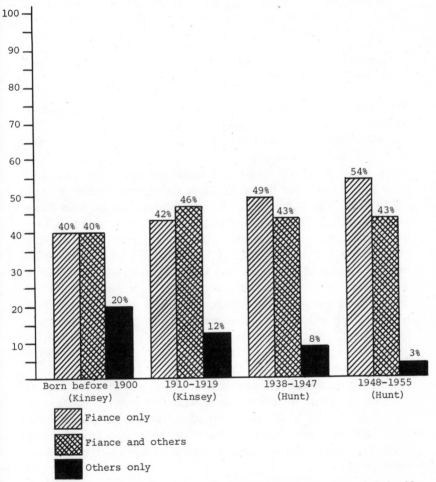

SOURCE: *Sexual Behavior in the 1970's* by Morton Hunt. Originally appeared in *Playboy* Magazine; copyright © 1973 by Morton Hunt. Reprinted by permission.

Virginia is a 63-year-old widow. Though she makes friends easily and has plenty of women friends, she misses male "companionship." Recently she read in the obituaries column in her local newspaper that a woman in her church had died and was survived by her husband. Virginia remembered him as a tall, nice-looking, refined gentleman who would be about 70 years old now. She wrote him a letter of condolence and invited him to supper at her home. He came bringing flowers and they had a wonderful time. Both admitted that they were lonely. He suggested that he move in with her. When she asked if he was proposing, he said emphatically, "No," they were too old for that. Virginia wants to let him move in, but is afraid of how her five adult children and twenty-four grandchildren will react.

The Cocktail Lounge Model. This type of relationship is described by Bernard as a semi-serious, semi-committed relationship, semi-stable; it is more than a transitory relationship, and generally lasts over a period of years. It is definitely not a pickup in the usual sense of this word. Typically, it is initiated in a locale not necessarily related to place of residence. For the young adult, the natural meeting place is apt to be the high-status cocktail lounge. Whereas, on the other hand, for the senior single the meeting place is usually the community center, a club, church, or shopping center. Sometimes, as among the young adults, the male may already be married. We pointed out earlier that the survival of a marriage into late life is no assurance that it is a happy and fulfilling one. In too many cases a spouse of many years has a chronic illness or is an invalid; or has been long turned off from sex. For these and many other reasons, a man is going to be reluctant to dissolve the marriage. Sometimes it may even be with the knowledge of his mate that the male establishes other relationships. These extra-marital relationships resemble the much discussed open-marriage concept. Given the disproportionate number of single women, this may be the only alternative for many women who want male friendships; or for a man thirsting for closeness. We have less reliable data on these kinds of relationships. Most of our information comes from housing managers, directors of community programs, and syndicated advice columns.

The Berkeley, Campus, or Companionship Model. This is the alternative Virginia wanted to adopt. It is the practice of men and women living together either before formal marriage or as a substitute for it. A more acceptable term for this model might be proto-family. Living together as unmarried couples has been the most popular alternative to marriage adopted by young people in the past decade. Or, at least, their openness about their living arrangement and their youth focused more attention on the young unmarried couples than on other adults. These are not frivolous, "touch-and-go" relationships. They are seriously undertaken and in many instances are almost Victorian in nature. But these neo-marital relationships have not been limited to the young. Landlords and housing managers report a surprising number of middle-aged couples who share apartments without benefit of clergy. The increase in the number of older persons living together is attributed more to social security and pension laws than an anti-establishment protest.

In 1960, for the first time, the Census Bureau began to gather data on persons by family characteristics, thus giving us for the first time information about neo-family types. There has been a sizable increase in primary individuals (a household head living alone or with non-relatives only) and households of unrelated individuals. Many of these households are of one sex, but the number which contain individuals of both sexes also has greatly increased.

Statistics released by the Internal Revenue Service in 1973 report a significant increase in the number of 65-year-old unmarried couples living together and filing returns.

Many of these couples, both young and old, view their living together as a "trial marriage." For whatever reason, this is an alternative that many adults choose. They find companionship—someone with whom to share, someone who cares. To continue intimate heterosexual relationships is a way of continuing to affirm one's sexuality identity and functionality.

From his study of 100 older couples sociologist Walter McKain concluded that the role of sex in the lives of older people extends far beyond lovemaking and coitus. A woman's gentle touch, the perfume of her hair, a word of endearment—all of these help satisfy a man's urge for the opposite sex. The same is true for the older woman—the little things such as the smell of his pipe, his shaving equipment, the sounds of his footsteps on the porch, and so on.

The most popular alternative to marriage for meeting these longings of single older adults is this unmarried couple model. The reason, as in the case of Virginia, is that some consider themselves too old for "traditional marriage," but they do want constant and intimate companionship on a live-in basis.

The Hippie Model. This alternative, developed during the 1960's, is the household with three or more unrelated individuals. Bernard describes them as "anti-Establishment" and a protest against the split-level life of many adults. This model tends to minimize the difference between the sexes and the relationship between them often looks more like a brother-sister than a loverly one. In a real sense this alternative, as it has been modified, represents an informal change in our monogamy standards. The incidence rate for what is so harshly characterized as "adultery" has been consistently growing since 1890. In one sense this may be interpreted as a loss of moral standards, of a surrender to sensuality; but in another sense it may be regarded as a functional adjustment of society's mores to the fact of the vast plurality of women. Certainly the evidence from Cuber and Harroff indicates that our distinguished men and women do not find emotional satisfaction in their marriages, but they stick to them, partly because they have other sexual relationships outside marriage.

This alternative suggests that many individuals in society are adopting a cover form of polygamy in which some men find a full life because of differential relationships with several women. Thus a man may find intellectual companionship with one woman, household tranquility with another, and sexual satisfaction with still a third. Certainly there are some men and women who can please each other on all levels, but this seems to be rare indeed. Furthermore, a couple may start out being quite well matched, but one member grows intellectually more than the other, or one grows old more rapidly than the other.

It would be an error to equate this new form of polygamy with the keeping of a mistress. The new form is based on the growing freedom of women and the unique social needs of the growing number of persons over the age of 60.

Dr. Victor Kassels, who has spent the major portion of his medical career in the practice of geriatrics, has found the greatest frustrations of older people arise as they try to fulfill their social necessities. As a solution to the unfulfilled social needs of the elderly he recommends a change to polygamy—a limited polygamy—after the age of 60. This would of course necessitate a change in our social philosophy or ethic. Many may consider this change to be radical, but Dr. Kassels reminds us that it is a *return* to a practice that at one time was considered proper in the Judeo-Christian ethic.

In addition to giving the women a chance to remarry, polygamy offers an opportunity to re-establish a meaningful family group. The health of these single persons would be expected to improve. It is a well-documented fact that most persons who live alone have an inadequate diet. Women with unused cooking skills would have the incentive to cook and to maintain a proper diet. Another positive benefit is related to illness. Many persons would not need nursing home care if responsible people at home were available. Many are hospitalized simply because they live alone and are unable to get home nursing care. In this arrangement housework would be shared and no one would have to be overworked.

In the area of sex—the most delicate and controversial aspect of this alternative—Dr. Kassels argues:

> Marriage sanctions sexual activity, and the polygynous marriage enables the unmarried older woman to find a partner. Most widows refrain from sex because they lack this partner; society has taught women to remain chaste when not married.
>
> To many people it is abhorrent to visualize grandparents or even parents past the childbearing stage enjoying the pleasure of sexual intercourse. Older women, recognizing this attitude, repress their sexual desires and develop psychological conflicts and consequent guilt. Studies have demonstrated, however, that most women have an increase in libido after the menopause simply because they lose the fear of pregnancy. A polygynous marriage enables them to express this desire, instead of remaining repressed through a continent widowhood.
>
> As for the men, sexologists claim that the male is polygynous by nature. The development of impotency and decreased libido in older men need not represent a senile change. The existence of a climacteric in the male has never been positively established. It seems that most impotency in the aged male represents boredom and many times an unattractive, uninterested partner. With variety, greater interest is sparked and many men can come back to life sexually. Also, the problem of the frigid wife is eliminated; other partners are available. Polygynous marriage offers a solution to a number of sexual problems of the aged.*

Perhaps one of the most significant contributions polygamy would make is to reduce the major psychiatric problems encountered by geriatricians—depression. Kassels believes that being a vital part of a family again, feeling useful and having people of similar interest to be with would reduce this problem dramatically.

* Reprinted with permission from "Polygyny After 60" by Victor Kassel, M.D. in *Geriatrics* 21, No. 4, pp. 214–218. Copyright The New York Times Media Company, Inc.

The change recommended by Dr. Kassels in view of the disproportion of men and women past the age of 55, that society should openly relax its laws of monogamy and countenance multiple wives or husbands is not likely to come about for a long time. Society has surrounded the family with the strictest of rules because the family is essential to the structure of society. That the reasons for those rules do not apply as stringently to people after childbearing years is a subtlety that society is not likely to appreciate for a great many years. But the possibility is being openly discussed. In a recent forum that dealt with widows one woman stated her position quite succinctly and it is the way many women feel: "I think that it is perfectly logical to change our marriage rules. I think we are going to have to have some form of polygamy or else many women are going to be deprived. But I do not want to share my husband. If he dies and I am widowed I may change my values."

For this alternative to become open—and approved—those of all ages socialized to monogamy will need to be resocialized to the benefits—particularly for those over age 60—of a polygynous family form.

The One Sex Community Model. This alternative is one in which singles eschew companionship with the opposite sex and depend rather exclusively on others of the same sex for their emotional satisfaction. This alternative includes those who seek companionship without intimate contact and those who seek sexual experiences of a homosexual or lesbian type.

At this point, we need to repeat that people have sexual tensions throughout their lives. Outlets vary throughout the life cycle with social situations, including marital status. Those who never marry and those who experience periods of singleness have the same sexual tensions and their outlets will include coitus, masturbation and erotic dreams.

Freud's concept of sublimation has become so much a part of our popular belief system that many friends, family and counselors of senior singles advise releasing sexual tension through other nonsexual physical activity such as volunteer work, club and religious activities, part-time work, and senior citizens' programs. Those with very low sexual tensions may find the heterosexual contacts in such activities sufficient and satisfying. We venture to predict, however, that for adults who have had years of meaningful sexual experience, involvement in such activities will serve more as a stimulus and revive the desire for a sex partner.

There are singles who turn to the same sex for companionship and sex partners. Some of these have always found their need for intimacy met by physical contact with others of the same sex. One of the consequences of the protests of the 1960's was to bring out into open this "gay" behavior of many adults. The gay protestors on college campuses and in the courts have won some rights and public acceptance (short of approval) for homosexual behavior. Again, most every adult has had a homosexual experience at some time in his life, but he does not consider himself to be gay. That this alternative becomes viable again in the later years should come as no great surprise any more than the increase in masturbatory behavior.

The inequities of the gay aged are pointed out in a recent report from an English group, the Committee for Homosexual Equality. The Committee reports that in England the over-60 age group is charged with 6 per cent of the indictable offenses, compared to less than 2 per cent of all indictable crimes. The majority of these offenses are homosexual. Furthermore, the Committee points out an elderly homosexual faces social as well as sexual problems. A widowed heterosexual may still have the comfort of a family or children. An elderly homosexual in the same situation does not have the same support. Such a study has not been made in the United States, but if one should be made we would expect the findings to be similar, if not higher. In addition to the legal punishment, the condemnatory attitude of society toward all forms of sexual satisfaction outside marriage increases the guilt and anxiety of the older single.

During the Middle Ages the unwanted and superfluous females ran to religious orders and found deep rewards in their religious vocations and in the warmth that came from other females. Today some females are turning to a modern version of the nunneries. In every large city there are living establishments for women as well as for men. Some women, but certainly not the majority, find their need for intimacy met by physical contacts with other women. We encounter all types and degrees of lesbian experience where the companionship has a physical component which is satisfying for some women and repulsive to others.

The case study that Dr. Arlie Hochschild, a sociologist, made of a senior citizen apartment complex in San Francisco provides us with reliable insights into this model. The residents included 37 women and 6 men. These women were conservative, religiously fundamentalist

from the Midwest and Southwest—very unlikely candidates for communal living and alternatives to the nuclear family. Although each resident lived in a single apartment, they had developed a communal
life-style which brought "order out of ambiguity—a set of obligations
to the outside community and to one another where few had existed
before." Aside from what Hochschild describes as a beehive of activity
—meetings of service clubs, bowling, Bible study classes and other
adult education classes, parties and visits to nearby nursing homes,
and so on—strong friendship networks have been established. In turn,
the friendship networks have developed into a particular kind of relationship called the "sibling bond."

Once again we have identified a similarity between the young and
the old. Both of those periods of life are better for forming sibling
bonds than are any other periods. Hochschild's observation was:

> Both just before starting a family and after raising one, before entering
> the economy and after leaving it, an individual is open to, and needs,
> these back-up relationships. It is these stages that are problematic, and
> it is these stages that, with longer education and earlier retirement, now
> last longer.*

This sisterhood both preserves the individuals' autonomy and provides companionship. In this predominantly one-sex community there
are many close intimates to share experiences of joy and grief, to
listen to problems, fears, and anxieties, to provide emotional support
and social reassurance. In the event of "normal sickness" these close
ones will look after each other and make it possible to prolong—or
perhaps avoid entirely—moving into a nursing home.

Hochschild evaluates the sibling bond as allowing more flexibility between generations by forging solidarity within generations and divi-
sions between them. The consequence for society, she says:

> . . . is to divide it into age layers that are relatively independent of one
> another, so that changes in one age layer need not be retarded by con-
> ditions in another. The institution that has bound the generations to-
> gether—the family—is in this respect on the decline. As it declines, the
> sibling bond emerges, filling in and enhancing social flexibility, espe-
> cially in those social strata where social flexibility does not guarantee
> "good" changes, and continuity is partly sacrificed to fads and a cult

* Arlie Russell Hochschild, *The Unexpected Community* © 1973. Reprinted by
permission of Prentice-Hall, Inc., Englewood Cliffs, N.J.

of newness. But whether desirable or not, this flexibility is partly due to, and partly causes, the growing importance of the sibling bond.*

We suppose that the cost of all experiments such as communes, and lesbian activity or polygamous behavior, has to be paid in the coin of secrecy and social condemnation. Certainly these experiments require a new type of openness and honesty between persons as well as high courage to so flout the older standards of perfection. Sometimes our case studies reveal that relationships which otherwise might achieve very high peaks of joy are shadowed by covertness and secrecy. On the other hand a great many individuals are openly living as they please. And in many of the cases we have studied, men and women of great sensitivity are determined that their joy cannot be allowed to hurt another human being but, at the same time, that the meaning they have for each other will not be denied.

We are, of course, neither recommending nor condemning any of these alternatives. Some readers who are stuck in the moral imperatives of yesteryear will undoubtedly wish we had blasted the innovators. But this is a new world of aging. Not all past patterns can be replicated in a highly healthy and technological world. In a sense, then, we must explore every alternative solution there is for the plight of those ten million women. This problem of the plurality of women over men is not going to go away; in fact, it may be come accentuated. What is needed is a fair evaluation of the possible rewards and/or dangers associated with each pathway to intimacy and love.

The Nursing Home Resident. Thus far we have assumed that these singles are socially and physically able to live autonomously in our neighborhoods and communities. Some 4 per cent of the 21 million persons over age 65, however, are in nursing homes or other health care facilities. And, as age increases, so does the percentage of persons entering long-term health care facilities. Some 14 per cent of those age 85 and over are residents of these homes. Most of these are single, female, and have been living alone. Those who have relatives to help care for them and/or have adequate incomes are able to avoid moving into nursing homes. As we pointed out, the communal alternatives provide older singles with the social support—the neo-family —that delays or removes entirely the necessity of entering such facilities.

Our concern here is with those who do enter health care facilities.

* *Ibid.*

There is nothing about entering a nursing home that should strip a person of his or her sexuality or personhood. The senior single will continue to have sexual tensions, memories, and the human need for intimate and loving bonds. Biologist Desmond Morris calls these needs "social bonds which range from eye to body to eye contact, touching of hands, shoulders, waist, head, to other private parts." He believes that from womb to tomb, touching is modern man's most urgent, most frustrated, and most misunderstood need. We will add only that it is more so for the elderly—and particularly for the elderly in nursing homes.

If society has little sympathy for the sex needs of those senior persons living in the community it has even less for those in nursing homes. Signs of sexual interest by residents or overt acts—whether heterosexual, homosexual, or masturbatory—are treated with horror by nurses and administrators.

A nursing home administrator came to us with what he considered a serious problem. A male resident who wandered and was not always "reality oriented," was physically well, neat and attractive. He liked the women and all the levels of contact. He was "caught" by a nurse with one of the female patients who was responding to his overtures. The administrator had scheduled a staff meeting to determine what action to take. He was seriously considering "expelling" the elderly man from the home.

We answered the administrator with a quote from Dr. Kassel's address to the Washington State Health Facilities Association in which he recommended intimate loving for these singles and observed that nursing home operators are too puritanical and project their own values on their residents. Kassel said, further, that elderly patients who have normal sexual appetites but are treated as though they shouldn't will show signs of emotional distress. To deny them is to contribute to the most common complaint of nursing home residents, depression. The nursing home administrator who claims there is no sexual activity in his facility is simply blind to reality.

The attitude toward sex in the nursing home is reflected in a joke that is popular among those who serve the elderly:

> In Eventide Nursing Home, the men and women residents gathered around the television set every evening. One of the female residents, Mary Beam, became bored with this evening ritual and decided to break it up. One evening as all were gathered around the tube, she took off her clothes and streaked down the hall past the viewers. No one looked

up. So she decided to streak back. Still no one looked up. Disgusted, she went back and stood between the TV set and one of the men. She asked, "Don't you notice anything?" After a pause, the man responded, "Yes, your dress needs ironing,"

We need nursing home administrators who understand the sex needs and expressions that will, and should be expected to, develop within the closed community of the nursing home. Opportunities for privacy and intimacy need to be socially and physically possible for their residents. As more administrators and nurses have courses in gerontology included in their training, we can expect these stereotypes about the intimate needs of nursing home residents to change. Many enlightened administrators are already taking appropriate action to improve the social opportunities of their residents.

Love in some social expression is necessary for life at every age. Love is the way through which the human infant finds sufficient strength for life and development. The studies of Erich Fromm, Arnold Gesell and Bruno Bettelheim indicate that infants who do not get cuddling, fondling, and loving are likely to lose weight, fret, whimper, and even die. Gerontologists are in agreement that the same is true for older adults. At the end, no less than at the beginning, the human individual needs love. Older persons who are denied the intimate social bonds lose their appetites, become depressed, fret, demand, withdraw. When older persons are free to continue to develop their capacities for love and to explore new social forms for living, their quality of life improves.

7

Economics and Social Involvement

Love may make the world go around, but it is money that greases the wheels. This bit of popular philosophy is an even harsher fact of life for older lovers than it is for young lovers. Psychological factors are so intermingled with the economic aspects of senior social bonds that we were compelled to mention three important economic areas: 1) the discussion of housing related to success of retirement marriage and the alternatives to marriage; 2) the question of the careful management of the estate had to do with the approval of adult children of their surviving parent's remarriage; and 3) the question of late marriage involved a discussion of social security payments and the loss of part of the widow's pension. Among the alternatives to traditional marriage we pointed out the economic advantages of some of the options for senior singles. Our quest for meaningful love relationships in the later years has brought us face to face with the crucial role of financial resources in developing and maintaining a social network of friends, neighbors and a family.

Older adult groups tell us that economic resources are their number-one concern. For most of the elderly the question of financial resources determines to what extent they can plan for a number of experiences, including travel, attending special events, belonging to clubs, entertaining friends, etc.; and for the singles—getting married. Certainly many of the programs for enriching social life involve some cost.

What makes the problem of financial resources unique for senior adults? To answer this question and to suggest some resources for coping with the problem we need to review what these resources are along with the sources of retirement income.

Financial Adequacy or Crisis?

Most adults in our society have to face the economic reality that they will live on a reduced income when they retire. What many of them are not prepared for, however, is how much less they will have and how much the cost of living will have increased. Older persons have less than half the income of younger persons. A survey conducted in March of 1973 revealed that the median income for a two-person aged household was $5,487 (or about $106 per week), compared with $11,861 (more than $228 per week) for a two-person household with a head in the age 25-44 category. These age differences in income are dramatically portrayed in Figure 13. It is based on the 1973 median family income.

Furthermore, older people do not have the same access or hope of access to ways of increasing their income that younger persons do. Many people believe this state of affairs is as it should be. They accept the myth that retired people do not need as much money as younger people because their children are grown and they do not have the inclination or the energy to participate in activities younger adults enjoy.

A more cheerful belief about the life of the retired person voiced by many adults is, "Now that you are retired, you have the time to do all the things you've been wanting to do!" But the *doing* involves *spending*. The time without the resources becomes a trap. As we shall see, the impact of retirement on financial resources and their adequacy ranges from minimal to crisis. Many face a reduction in their level of living. Others find they are poor for the first time in their lives. The elderly are paying a high personal price for vast economic changes not of their making.

The major sources of income for older people are from Social Security, pensions, and Old Age Assistance. While it is discouraging to project a continuing and increasing inflation, the financial forecasts for the mid-Seventies are that inflation and the rising cost of living will continue. Except for social security, most pensions are figured on a strict dollar limit, and inflation means that every month older persons get less and less real money. Social security is now tied to the

FIGURE 13

Age When Earnings Hit Peak

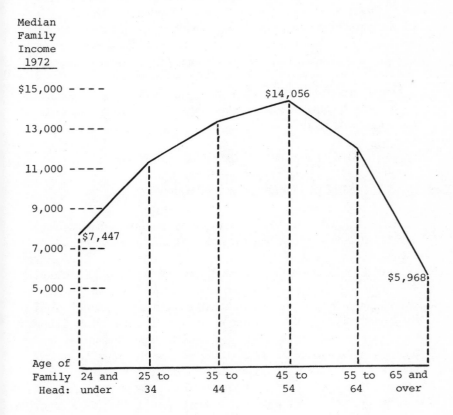

SOURCE: Reprinted from *U.S. News & World Report,* August 20, 1973, p. 39. Copyright 1973 U.S. News & World Report, Inc.

inflation spiral, however, so that payments are adjusted whenever the dollar's value is decreased by 5 per cent.

One of the best friends and public advocates older people have is the United States Senate Committee on Aging. This Committee investigates the needs and problems of older people and recommends legislation to help solve them. The Committee's monthly Bulletin is available, without charge. You may request it directly from the Committee or from either of your state's two U.S. Senators. This Committee recognized that older persons on fixed incomes suffer most during periods of financial turmoil. The Committee also knew that the cost of living was climbing fast and recommended the 11 per cent increase in social security benefits passed by Congress in 1974.

Despite the cost-of-living adjustments and increases in Supplemental Security Income, the average monthly social security income for retired persons in 1974 was:

> $181 per month for the typical retired worker
> $310 per month for a retired couple
> $177 per month for an aged widow.

These fall below the poverty level and the assumption is that the older person has other assets and sources of income to make up the difference.

Marital status is a major income differential among older persons. The older woman is most likely to be single and living on less! Discrimination against women in company insurance and pension plans has been brought to the attention of the U.S. Department of Labor by several women's groups. The Department found that many companies do differentiate in the amount paid per month to the retired man and to a retired woman under the same provisions. Insurance experts argue that sex cannot be removed as a factor in figuring insurance and retirement programs because women live longer than men. In some companies women receive equal pensions overall, but smaller monthly payments in order to make their retirement benefits stretch over their anticipated longer life span. Conversely, men may receive less insurance coverage because they do not live long enough to collect it. No one argues against the fact that women live longer than men. But while the single men and women are living, the women suffer economically more than do the men. Dr. Norma K. Raffel of Women's Equity Action League observes that the cost of a bag of groceries or apartment rent is absolutely the same for men and women, but the woman still gets the lower pension and insurance benefits. The single man, then, is more likely to have a higher monthly income than the single woman.

Some older people are well off. As Figures 14 and 15 show, 17 per cent (or about 850,000 couples over 65) had incomes of $10,000 in 1971, and 13 per cent (or 790,000 single persons) had incomes of $5,000 or more. But many are not so well off. Half of the older families had incomes of less than $5,000. The median income of older persons living alone or with nonrelatives was $2,397.

It is encouraging that the real income of older persons has increased to the extent that while 25 per cent of them were on an income below the poverty level in 1960, this figure had been reduced to about 20 per cent in 1971. A recent report of the Senate Committee on Aging (1973) points out that the 3.7 million of the elderly living below the poverty level in 1974 is an improvement over the 5 million in 1970. Increased social security benefits may be the primary reason for this improvement. However, that still leaves 3.7 million persons in a condition that can hardly be described as "the best that is" or very graceful!

In a recent study of financial adequacy David Peterson, of the Institute of Gerontology at the University of Michigan, found that retirees perceive their finances as inadequate and their financial position as deteriorating. Fixed incomes and unfixed prices add up to financial crisis for the retired.

Food, housing, transportation and medical care account for the bulk of expenditures for most older Americans. The most recent Bureau of Labor Statistics Intermediate Budget for a retired couple allocates about 80 per cent (or $4 out of every $5) for these four essential items.

Sylvia Porter, the New York financial analyst, observes that inflation hits older people hardest because it erodes the value of a lifetime of retirement savings and reduces the buying power of fixed-income pension and other benefits—particularly in the case of such necessities as home maintenance, insurance, taxes, public transportation and medical care.

Medicare is a help, but it covers less than half the total health costs. Some especially important needs are not covered by Medicare, such as dental work, hearing aids, eyeglasses and out-of-hospital care. Also, it does not cover preventive medical care and much of the care required for the chronic illnesses which afflict 85 per cent of the older

FIGURE 14

Income Distribution of 5 Million Couples with Heads 65 and Over, 1971*

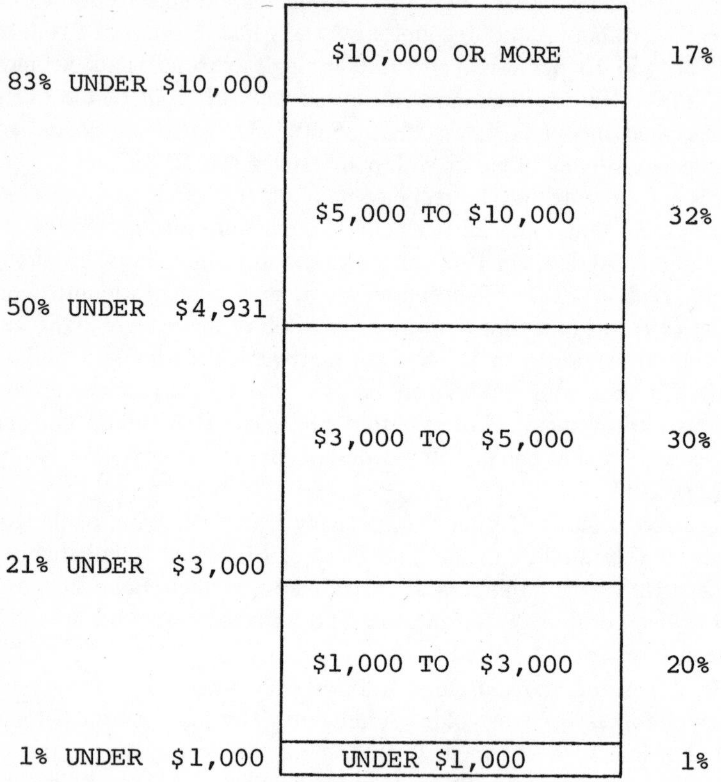

83% UNDER $10,000	$10,000 OR MORE	17%
	$5,000 TO $10,000	32%
50% UNDER $4,931		
	$3,000 TO $5,000	30%
21% UNDER $3,000		
	$1,000 TO $3,000	20%
1% UNDER $1,000	UNDER $1,000	1%

*Income data is tabulated by age of head of family or of a person living alone or with nonrelatives. Data presented above represent only couples (2-person husband-wife· families) or individuals living alone or with nonrelatives to avoid factors introduced by presence of family members of other ages.

SOURCE: *New Facts About Older Americans,* U.S. Department of Health, Education and Welfare, June, 1973.

FIGURE 15

Income Distribution of 6.1 Million Persons Aged 65 and Over, Living Alone or With Nonrelatives, 1971*

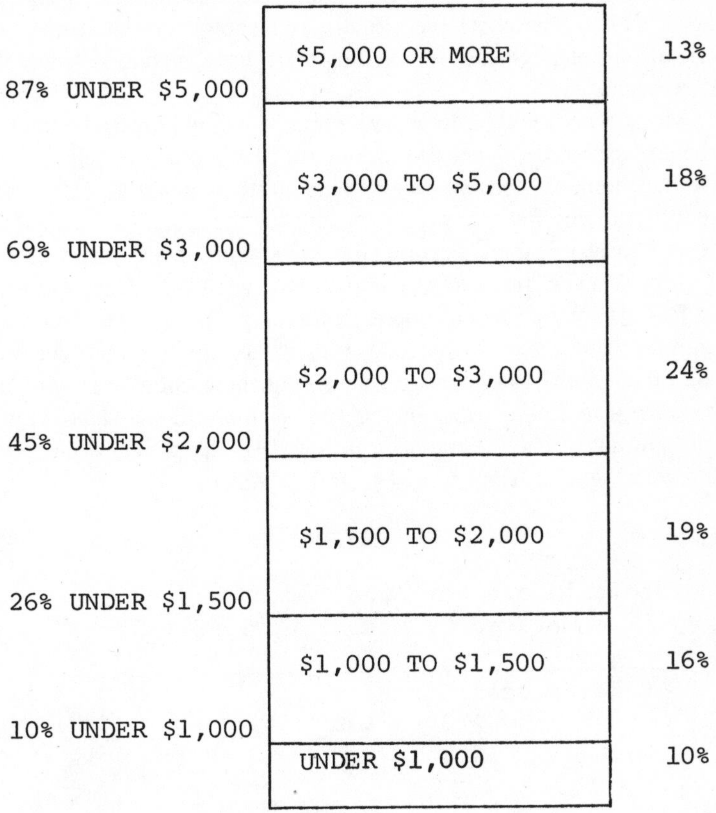

87% UNDER $5,000	$5,000 OR MORE	13%
69% UNDER $3,000	$3,000 TO $5,000	18%
45% UNDER $2,000	$2,000 TO $3,000	24%
26% UNDER $1,500	$1,500 TO $2,000	19%
10% UNDER $1,000	$1,000 TO $1,500	16%
	UNDER $1,000	10%

*Income data is tabulated by age of head of family or of a person living alone or with nonrelatives. Data presented above represent only couples (2 person husband-wife families) or individuals living alone or with nonrelatives to avoid factors introduced by presence of family members of other ages.

SOURCE: *New Facts About Older Americans*, U.S. Department of Health, Education and Welfare, June, 1973.

persons not in a hospital or nursing home. Given reasonable medical attention and support systems, most (95 per cent) of those over the age of 65 can avoid entering the hospital or some long-term-care institution. The Social Security Administration reports that in 1973 Medicare covered only 40.3 per cent of the total health bill of $1,040 per aged person. The chart (see Figure 16) shows how these per capita out-of-pocket payments for medical care have increased since Medicare began.

Many who thought they had planned wisely for retirement find themselves being pauperized. Some are being forced to sell the equity in their home. When apartment rents go up as much as $15 to $20 a month, moving into nonprofit housing for the elderly or going to live with family members become the only alternatives. Art Carney as "Harry," in the movie *Harry and Tonto,* vividly portrays the trauma of forced moving for the retired, autonomous person. He found living with his family was "no good" for them nor for him. Neither he nor the other older Americans are accepting these conditions with indifference. The finest scene in the film is the one in which Harry is brought out of his apartment in his chair by the police, while protesting with vigor at being forced from his home.

FIGURE 16

Medical Care Per Aged Person and Proportion
Covered by Medicare, 1966-1973

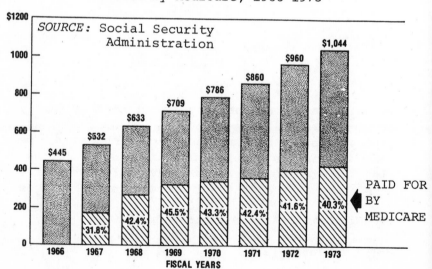

Some problems in respect to inadequate income are shown in this 1974 Miami Beach news story:

> Unless Miami Beach forces thousands of impoverished elderly residents off South Beach and uses the land to rescue rapidly declining tourism, the playground city faces economic strangulation, according to a just-released report, based upon an in-depth survey. But nobody seems to know what to do about South Beach's 29,000 old folks, half of them trying to exist on incomes below the poverty level.
>
> Said *Miami News* editor Jim Fain in his editorial page column: "...There is a human tragedy pending on the kind of monumental scale that qualifies as catastrophe."
>
> The survey, made by Albert Rosen Associates, a Miami Beach consulting firm, said that tourists are "shrinking in number. New tourist developments, including hotels (none has built since 1967), are a prerequisite in rejuvenating the faltering industry." Shepard Davis, president of the Tenants Association of Florida, said he doubted the feasibility of establishing a redevelopment authority with a resultant multimillion-dollar bond offering. Davis was sharply critical of the city, declaring: "The city has had the chance for five years now (since the 1969 master plan) to build a lousy 200 units of low-cost housing, and they haven't done it yet. The old people are being pushed from pillar to post. The city is, frankly, going to get rid of them, one way or the other."
>
> Sharply rising costs for such essentials as rent and food, have reached a level where they exceed the income of many of the South Beach residents, the Rosen report said. The report said the elderly are left with two alternatives: either decrease rent or decrease food consumption, but since almost all are unable to lower their rents they have to eat less food ... or steal it, or raid garbage cans.
>
> In the 1966 master plan, it was pointed out that if Miami Beach was to have its tourist industry, the ever-older age trend of its population would have to be reversed. The city's median age increased from 43 years in 1950 to 59 years in 1966, and the aging trend has continued. The Rosen report said that the median age on South Beach is 68 now. "One of Miami Beach's goals," the report said, "is to reverse the aging trend by encouraging younger, middle-income families and persons to reside in Miami Beach."
>
> The Rosen consultants found "some truth" in the opinion prevalent on Miami Beach that the "influx of senior citizens has succeeded in discouraging middle-income younger families and individuals from residing in the area." But, the report conclude, the city can resolve the problem: It can relocate present residents off the South Beach land, and it can keep future poor folks from moving in by taking the tiny, mostly

single rooms and efficiency apartments off the rental market when they become vacant.

Groups of senior citizens are organizing all over the country to use political power at all levels of government to get what they need to live in dignity and to preserve what they earned during their working years. Such organizations as the National Retired Teacher's Association and the American Association of Retired Persons have over 7 million members. They maintain a lobbyist in Washington, and many of their members serve as lobbyists in state and local governments.

Social Security Administration regulations limit the possibilities for improvement in the financial conditions of those over age 65. In addition to being penalized by reduced benefits if they marry, older persons are restricted in the amount of work they can do without paying a penalty. The annual earnings limitation discourages those under age 72 who are still capable of working from doing so. In 1974 these regulations were liberalized: For earnings in excess of $2,400 (up from $1,600) $1.00 in benefits would be withheld for each $2.00 of wages. This so-called liberalization seems strange to us. It seems more like denial of the right to work of those over age 62. If social security is insurance for which the worker has paid monthly premiums, why should he be limited in his extra earnings if he has the opportunity and inclination to work, any more than if it were interest on a savings account or private pension? This is another one of those areas for political action by the millions of adults affected now plus those who will be discovering these unhappy facts each year.

Despite the limitations, some older adults do work. More than 3 million (or about 16 per cent of those over age 65) are in the labor force and make up 3.4 per cent of the United States labor force. The "double standard" is evident in work opportunities after retirement. More older men (2 million) than older women work. The Department of Health, Education, and Welfare reports that the male labor force participation rates have decreased steadily from two in three older men in 1900, to one in four in 1972. The female rate has risen slightly from one in twelve in 1900 to one in ten in 1972. Not only do fewer retired persons work but the jobs available are usually the lower-paid ones.

The problem of working has more than economic consequences, if the meaning of work is involved in defining our self-worth and self-esteem. Arthur N. Swartz, psychologist at the Ethel Percy Andrus

Gerontology Center, in writing about the effects of retirement, points out that the business community tends to see retirement as a method of control, *e.g.,* getting rid of "deadwood," making room for younger workers, etc. He does not believe that industrial management is nearly so imaginative and creative as it might be about work roles for older persons, possibly because it does not yet fully appreciate how closely the meaning and importance of the individual's work is related to his sense of self-worth.

Some older persons are trying to break the age barrier in order to work. A small but determined group of educators, for example, are telling schools to keep their retirement gifts and titles and give them back their jobs. They do not think age should be the sole criterion for filling a job. They want to work as long as they are productive. The American Civil Liberties Union is offering them sympathy and backing in several suits, whose status nationally is as follows:

The State Supreme Court in Hawaii likely will rule this year on whether to uphold or deny a lower court decision that Frank Nelson, a professor of English at Hilo College, a branch of the University of Hawaii, cannot be forced to retire at age of 65. The university requirement violates the equal protection clause of the U.S. Constitution, the court said, because other state and county employees don't have to retire until age 70. Last year, a lower court held in favor of Nelson but also pointed out that age ceilings for public employees are not "prohibited per se" and that the university did not discriminate in applying its retirement policy.

. . . .

ACLU attorneys in Chicago plan to appeal a Federal court decision that the forced retirement of Julia Gault, a 65-year-old Lansing, Ill., biology teacher, was not a denial of equal protection, an infringement of a fundamental right, or an improper government interest. "It [age 65] has long been accepted as an age when most people, because of diminishing mental and physical stamina, are no longer able to endure the rigors of full-time employment," said the court.

. . . .

Joseph Rosen, 62-year-old superintendent of School District 10 in Chicago, has asked a Federal court to find that the Illinois school code requiring retirement at age 65 is unconstitutional because it discriminates against and denies due process to one age class. ACLU attorneys have charged that Rosen will be "stigmatized" and "will suffer . . . physical and mental harm to his well-being" if he is forced to retire. The case will be decided later this year.

Howard Eglit, the Chicago ACLU attorney handling the Gault and Rosen cases, has put together a "rights of the elderly" project and maintains that a person who has worked all his life has earned a "right to work" and should not be fired without a hearing. He maintains that much like criminals in prison, the elderly who are abruptly deprived of work develop mental disorders because of becoming the "dumping ground of human hopes."

Some older persons are exploring alternative career plans for retirement as a new and perhaps different, but still satisfying, way to spend the last decades of life. One of the graduate students in our Gerontology Degree program is a woman in her mid-sixties. She has the educational background for the work and years of experience as a volunteer in nursing homes. She plans to continue working in some of the programs for the elderly or in a nursing home. Some older persons, become "ill" before they find their new way to retire, as illustrated in the following case study:

Dr. P. is a ruddy-faced, silver-haired, hearty-looking man in his early 60's who came for counseling because of increasingly frequent physical symptoms: some insomnia, daytime restiveness, sundry aches and pains in his extremities, and a tendency toward occasional brief blackouts. Examination by his personal physician indicated no clear physical cause. Dr. P. had for many years maintained a highly successful, independent dental practice in an upper-middle-class resort community in which he was well known, liked and respected. He was a man of some consequence in his profession, having served on state boards and taught at a local university dental school. Now tired of long workweeks, he was serious about retiring and thus eager to find just the right assistant to take over his practice. Because of his stipulations that the assistant be above average in skill, highly ethical, able to maintain the loyalty of an affluent, devoted clientele, and the like, finding a likely candidate was not an easy task. In fact, Dr. P. attributed his symptoms almost wholly to the stress generated by his need to get out of his arduous practice and his difficulty in finding a suitable replacement.

The more this matter was explored in counseling, the more it became evident that these problems were not the prime source of his intrapsychic stress. Nor did his distress have to do with family relations, which apparently were excellent. The crux of the matter began to emerge during the third counseling session, when Dr. P. verbalized his apprehensions about becoming a cipher, a nonentity, a golf-course hanger-on after his retirement. Having long been active in a career that offered him much evidence of his own effectiveness and impact, he could not tolerate the idea of becoming in effect a shadow of this former self. Underlying his manifest distress and symptoms was the fact that his self-esteem was at stake. He clearly felt he had little of consequence to retire to.

Subsequent counseling sessions explored several available options. The most appealing and satisfying to him was the possibility of doing direct teaching, on a preceptor basis, with a few dental students for limited periods. This was an activity and a role that he had much enjoyed in the past and that promised a great deal of satisfaction through the use of his warm manner, his considerable expertise, and his enormous amount of experience.

We agree that our society cannot long tolerate, either spiritually or economically, an ever-increasing number of overly dependent adults required to live in personal oblivion as public charges. All of us who hope to survive into our later years want the surviving to be worthwhile.

Housing

Just as with the problems of work for the elderly discussed above, the problem of housing has not only a financial aspect but also a socio-psychological aspect. Many individuals have found that the increasing tax burden has often made it impossible for them to live in their beloved family homes. Others have found that a house which was comfortable when three or four children were about has become too large for the smaller amount of energy they can expend on maintenance. Older men often enjoy keeping up large lawns and gardens, but as the years pass this task becomes overwhelming, and they look for alternatives. Neighborhoods change. Neighbors cherished over the years die or move so that time means isolation. Sometimes, too, they discover that the church is too far away; so is the bank or the golf course—and distance discourages participation and/or shopping. All of these factors need to be taken into account when housing decisions are made.

There are now many alternative living arrangements for retired persons. Some elect to live in mobile or motor homes so that they can move from one part of the country to another. Others elect to live in one of the many retirement communities with service, recreational and religious institutions close at hand. They like to have planned programs for sociability and leisure-time activities that go with the purchase or rental of a home or apartment. In many cases more friends from yesteryear are found in one of the retirement homes than in the old neighborhoods. Still others stay in their old communities, but move to smaller apartments located closer to facilities they need. Like ev-

erything else, moving costs are high. So are taxes on the profit from
the sale of one's home. Inflation may seem to be a benefit when one
sells a home bought in the depression years at today's inflated prices,
but most people find they are unable to obtain comparable housing
with the profit. Moving is expensive and consumes much time and
energy.

Selecting a place to live may also have to do with one's family.
Many older people move to communities where their children are located. This way of coping with the mobility of adult children has the
built-in hazard that the children, who are at the peak of their careers,
may also be mobile, and it may not be possible for the parents to
move every time the children are transferred. There is the couple who
sold their home in Wisconsin and moved within twenty-five miles of
their son in Florida, only to have him move in three months to California. Older persons need to be particularly resistant to overly attractive housing investments or purchases. All the skills in decision-
making developed over the years need to be exercised during such a
retirement decision.

Taxes

Older people are taxpayers. In 1972 over 9 million tax returns were
filed by persons over age 65. It has been estimated by the Senate Committee on Aging that about one-half of these 9 million may have paid
more taxes than legally required. Individual tax returns are more complicated for older than for younger taxpayers. In many cases it is the
complexity that baffles and results in overpayment by persons who
can least afford it. In other cases the individuals are not aware of deductions which could save them many dollars. To avoid this overpay-
ing and to assure the older taxpayer that he has fulfilled his citizen's
obligation, tax counseling services are needed. Private ones, of course,
cost money. Senator Frank Church, Chairman of the Senate Committee on Aging, is concerned about tax overpayment. Under his leadership the Committee has prepared a helpful checklist of deductions to
aid the older taxpayer, special provisions for the aged, and information about tax counseling assistance. A copy of this checklist can be
secured by writing the United States Government Printing Office,
Washington, D.C., 20402. Enclose 35 cents for Document #27-5980
"Protecting Older Americans Against Overpayment of Income Taxes."

A free, nation-wide tax counseling service is offered by the Institute of Lifetime Learning, a continuing education joint program of
NRTA/AARP who describe the programs as follows:

Voluntary counseling for retired taxpayers in cooperation with the U.S. Internal Revenue Service. During the 1972-73 tax season the service provided 2,500 counselors who assisted more than 100,000 taxpayers in 625 cities.

Administered by the Institute's Washington, D.C., headquarters, the Tax-Aide service provides older volunteers throughout the country who have been trained by the Internal Revenue Service to deal specifically with retirement tax problems. While counselors are not tax preparers who fill out an individual's return, they meet individually with Tax-Aide participants to advise them of special tax considerations for which they are eligible and to counsel them on such tax ramifications as:

Tax filing regulations, new tax forms.

Social Security, pensions, annuities, stocks, bonds, savings, inheritances.

Sale of residence, capital gains.

Medicare and medical and drug expenses.

Deductions for dentures, eyeglasses, hearing aids, orthopedic shoes, braces.

Retirement income credit.

The NRTA/AARP Tax-Aide service is open to all older retired persons as a public service of the Associations.

For those persons who have substantial estates, careful planning as to their distribution can bring additional rewards from one's lifetime earnings. The Tax-Aide service or a good commercial tax consultant can help with these decisions. Many older Americans have found new roles and meaning in their lives as they established foundations or supported projects that help others plan for or solve the many economic and personal problems that occur in later life.

Consumerism and Frauds

Deceptive or shoddy marketing practices affecting the elderly have been receiving increasing attention at national and local levels. Both the Federal Trade Commission and the United States Postal Service have issued special publications meant to inform the older consumer about pitfalls in the marketplace. Some of the schemes can be considered dangerous, as well as false and misleading. Such was the case when one company in particular claimed to have developed a plan that, if followed, would cure the flu overnight, was a means of preventing oral cancer, would assist in extending the average age to 100 years, prevent many maiming diseases, and still cost less than $25. The Postal Inspection Service is increasing its public education and fraud-preventive programs at this time in a continuing effort to stamp out frauds.

Other warnings issued as a result of U.S. Postal Service investigations include:

- —fraudulent solicitation of funds,
- —work-at-home schemes "involving an infinite variety of products and/or services to be manufactured, sold, or performed in the home,"
- —home improvement promotional campaigns and the possibility "that *an upsurge in the questionable sale of furnaces, insulation, etc., will be seen due to the present energy crisis*" (emphasis added),
- —questionable business opportunities including distributorships, franchises, vending machines and other lures to investors. The report adds: "Retired and disabled persons lead the list of individuals who are preyed upon each year to 'put their savings to work and supplement their incomes.'"
- —Land sale swindles, although "concerted attention" within recent years has reduced their numbers.
- —Matrimonial schemes directed at lonely people, including the elderly.

One woman told about her experience, born out of her loneliness and sexual deprivation. She answered a computer mating ad and paid the fee of $200. The company matched her up—a 68-year-old Baptist widow with a 55-year-old Jewish man. Needless to say, neither was happy. The woman had the energy, fired by humiliation and anger, to take her case to the local Better Business Bureau and consequently was reimbursed. Others may not have been so fortunate.

Retirement years are not the time to relax the exercise of caution in the marketplace. The skills developed over the years in purchasing and managing one's financial affairs need to be utilized. Since so many of those making consumer decisions will be women, many of whom have depended upon others for major financial decisions, there is a great need for adult education courses and TV courses on money management, with the needs of older women emphasized. Younger women need to include preparation for family finances in their educational objectives.

One of the most difficult tasks for the retired couple is the adjustment to a greatly reduced income. Careful retirement planning helps couples plan for the fifteen or twenty years ahead, for further inroads of inflation, and for allocation of resources to high-priority plans. This will be discussed in more detail in the next chapter. If older couples do not plan well, in the first years of retirement they may have to dip into capital that ought to be carefully averaged over the rest of their days. They must also pay attention to the needs of the surviving partner, if there is provision in a pension plan that the pension is to terminate or diminish on the death of the primary pension holder.

In this sense the preparation of budgets for one year, five years and twenty years makes eminently good sense. These budgets will be correlated with the late-life plan that is suggested in the next two chapters. Although the economic changes of the 1970's make such budgeting difficult, it is still one of the best ways to assure the proper use of one's resources. Money is not the most important item in retirement planning, but without its careful administration many more important aspects of creative living cannot be realized.

In concluding this chapter, we will suggest something to do about the economic situation facing the retired person.

First. Older Americans should exercise their citizenship rights. Write to your representative in the U.S. Congress and state legislature as well as to your local officials. Join with groups who are pressing for changes in the laws that affect older people. Such groups include NRTA/AARP, the National Council on Aging, Maggie Kuhn's Gray Panthers, and others.

Second. Keep informed. Write for Government reports that keep you informed. Call the Federal agencies that can provide needed information about benefits available to you—in transportation, banking, drugs, housing, and recreation. Regarding this latter, music lovers should know that many city symphonies make free tickets available to retired persons. Some states give them free tuition so they can attend university classes or adult education courses. And the list of these benefits is steadily growing.

In the process of involvement you will find some very significant political and civic work that needs to be done. There are millions of people over the age of 65 who can do this work and do it well because they have the time and they know, firsthand, what the problems and needs of older persons are.

8

Planning for the Years Ahead

Planning for any couple can begin by making an inventory of their basic interests and potentialities for growth. But such an inventory is useless unless it galvanizes the couple into planning some concrete steps by which to move off a dull equilibrium and into adventure. A plan is an outline of expectations. We have analyzed the shock that comes with the realization that a standard of living requires drastic change when income is only one-half or one-third of what it has been. This means that careful budgeting is essential both economically and in terms of realizing the activities we may project as important. But energy, too, is often in short supply. Consequently, if the good life is to be realized, there must be less impulsivity and a more careful allocation of resources and energy. Trips can still be a part of your life. Celebrations must not be overlooked. Recreation should be included. But all these must now be more deliberately arranged in terms of time, money and strength, and this means planning—deliberate, careful planning. Let us follow the experience of a couple over the past six years as they face retirement.

Mary and Jim Jones appeared in my office to consult about their retirement plans. They had an admirable picture of their finances and their needs, so that the conversation tended to focus on the way they could use these resources to meet their needs. Mary was an enthusiastic and competent artist. Through the years she had taught classes in art

121

and exhibited in many significant exhibitions. She needed money to travel because she was a landscape artist. She had traveled over Mexico, Canada, Europe and the United States and she said she would find a sedentary life very dreary. She wondered if their reduced income could in some way be stretched to provide for travel. At the same time she needed a studio. Jim had been a sportsman all his life; he loved to hunt, to fish, to golf. He felt that these activities were important to his morale as he retired.

Inquiry revealed that the two had taken separate trips in the past. Jim had gone to Alaska for big-game hunting and Mary had gone to Canada. But that was when Jim was at the peak of his earning capacity. They would now have about $800 a month and such trips were impossible. However, when they had established a basic budget it was possible to plan with them one major trip a year together. They would make more modest plans. Instead of insisting on Alaska, Jim would fish and hunt in Montana and Mary could paint there. In their early life they had used a tent, but when they were more affluent each had stayed in a motel or hotel. Now they decided to invest in a small camper. This would enable them to make economical small trips during the year and then use it on their major trip. They planned to finance the camper as part of a general plan to sell their large house and get a smaller apartment. It was suggested to them that they might well investigate one of the retirement communities where they could live comfortably in a small apartment—a community which had a golf course and a community art studio. It was pointed out that these retirement communities also had educational programs and activities which would supplement their basic interests. They were given a list of such retirement facilities and they planned on visiting a number of them to see if they would like this type of living.

Later, at a follow-up session, they reported that they had sold their home, arrived at a budget something like the one planned together and were moving into a retirement community and buying a camper. However, they injected an exclamation that seems important to mention here. They were moving to the retirement community not only because of the golf course, art studio, educational classes and cost but also because the community provided upkeep of grounds and many supports for health and good living. They recognized that they would have more time for enjoyment of life if they cut down on other calls on their energy. Consequently they made the decision to move into that type of community.

In studies of retirement housing we have found that there is no one housing plan that satisfies every group of older persons. Some elect to move into retirement facilities; others stay in their communities;

many of the more mobile persons move to a trailer court and spend their winters in a warm climate and their summers in the north. Some move close to their children, and others go farther away. There is no pattern. But we did discover that older persons differ just as much as persons in their twenties, and that they are happiest when they select a mode which fits their basic interests and life-style. A place is significant *only* insofar as it enables us to play the roles we wish to play.

Thus planning involves a life inventory of interests and needs. Jim and Mary worked together to satisfy both. Single persons have a more difficult task because they have to choose their locale and housing arrangements not only to be sure their needs are met, but to ensure some possibility of closeness with other persons. Jim and Mary were aware that they would have limited energy and so they chose a location in which many things were going to be done for them so that they could use their energy in doing the things they really wanted to do.

But what do older persons really want to do? We have counseled literally hundreds of older couples who welcomed retirement so that they could use their leisure time in pursuit of some very special interest like fishing or gardening, or church. But in many of these cases before the first year was over they were bored and frustrated. The interests were excellent when they were peripheral and gave contrast to work, but when indulged in all the time they soon brought boredom. One caution we have learned is that much pre-retirement enthusiasm dissipates soon if there is not a balance in life between recreation, sociability, learning and service.

It is probably essential for most persons facing retirement to spend a long time talking with a mate, a counselor, or a friend about the future. In the crucible of honest probing it is possible to find out something about ourselves and then something about the kind of plans which we ought to make for the future. We well remember Jack and Jennifer who came to us after a year of retirement:

> Jack opened the conference by declaring his utter disillusionment with retirement. He had anticipated the freedom from work so that he could sleep late, read his newspaper in leisure, spend more time with Jennifer and, when he wished, play golf with his friends. His retirement started well and he was pleased with his routine. But he soon added forty pounds of weight and did less and less. Jennifer stated that as he added weight and became more indolent he also became more irritable. They began to quarrel incessantly and a good marriage of for-

ty years seemed to be dissolving. Jack wanted to know what had gone wrong. In the weeks that followed we explored his feelings about himself and discovered, as with many others, that he was not doing anything of which he could be proud. Nothing he was doing justified his existence. He said, "Every day I felt like I was wasting myself." Jennifer had continued her community interests and was likewise dissatisfied that Jack did nothing with his abilities. At that point we began to explore the things that might make Jack feel his last years were not being "wasted." He elected to find part-time work, rather than follow his wife into volunteer service. For him this was essential, and he found a job in which his lifelong training enabled him to feel he was making a contribution.

Many communities are developing counseling centers where couples can participate in pre-retirement planning. Some industries have these centers; many community colleges are developing them; a few private therapists have now had training in helping persons plan the last half of their lives. NRTA/AARP take a special interest in this field, and if you cannot find counseling facilities in your local area, write to them, and ask them to recommend persons or programs that will help. Their magazine, *Dynamic Maturity,* is designed to constantly bring resources and models before those from 50 to 65 years of age and older which will help in such planning.

Planning in the Face of Inflation

There is more to the previous story, because that first conference was held with Mary and Jim Jones over five years ago. They came back five years later full of fear and trembling. Two significant things had happened to our planning in the five years. The first and ugly one was inflation. In five years the dollars they had saved and were receiving had lost 40 per cent of their value. It was as though a thief had come into their home at night and lifted 40 per cent of their savings . . . only it was worse than that because it was 40 per cent of their life plan that was being taken away. Inflation is a thief. It robs persons who are on fixed pensions, on dividends, on any kind of interest. Men and women who have planned for a lifetime and set aside an ample reserve for their retirement suddenly find that their whole life plan has dissolved. Mary and Jim were not stupid; they had invested their savings quite wisely and they were still getting the returns . . . the problem was, and is, that the value of those returns had shriveled.

The Consumer Price Index (CPI) measures average changes in prices of goods and services usually bought by urban wage earners and clerical workers. It is based on the price of about 400 items, in 39 major statistical areas. A market basket of goods and services bought by urban wage earners and clerical workers has risen from $10.00 in 1967 to $15.19 in 1974. This is obviously a 50 per cent increase in cost, and pension dollars have shrunk accordingly.

Inflation is the number-one concern of anyone who retires. No matter how carefully he may have planned for economic security rampant inflation can reduce security to poverty. What had happened to Mary and Jim was obvious. As costs rose so did their rent, their food, their taxes, their transportation costs. They found their standard of living cut and their careful plans for future trips sabotaged. They asked what they could do as a hedge against inflation.

In combating inflation there are a number of planning guides which it seems important to mention. They may not be applicable to every situation, but so long as pension plans operate with no respect for the value or lack of value of the dollar we shall probably have this problem with us. There are a great many suggestions by economists which are calculated to ameliorate the national and international financial problems, but as we write this chapter retail prices are still rising and are now running at a rate of 11 per cent increase for the year. A hedge against inflation has to be on an individual basis, but here are a few suggestions that will help while we are hoping for some emergency action on the part of the Federal Government to protect our older citizens. The following suggestions have helped some people:

1. *Wise buying.* One studies the seasons and buys when supply is ample. A few suggestions will suffice: Corn in early spring is a luxury, but in the middle of summer is relatively economical. The cost of automobile tires is astronomical. For our car the standard price for a good, non-steel-belted tire is now fifty dollars, but on sale the same tire is thirty-six dollars. The vacation season means a rise in motel room costs, etc., but May, early June, and the middle of September have the same, if not better, weather, and the costs are much reduced. We figure that we live on the same level as our neighbors and friends, but for about 25 per cent less because of wise buying.

2. *Have a garden.* Fortunately the retirement community in which Jim and Mary live has set aside some acres for gardens by residents. As we worked out costs they became enthused over a garden. At the

end of summer when they gathered in their harvest they figured that they had been able to save at least 400 dollars by living out of their garden. They did have a problem in trying to figure out where to store their carrots and potatoes; but they worked that out, too, and Mary learned to can the vegetables their freezer wouldn't hold. What turned out to be the serendipitous result was that Jim, who had never gardened before, got real joy from growing things. It became a new hobby with him as well as a profitable one.

3. *Learn home repair.* When Jim was working he was too busy ever to fix a toilet or repair a hinge on the door. As we looked at their last year's expenses it became apparent that quite a sum of money had been spent on small repair jobs. We were not very hopeful about doing anything about this, because though Jim was developing a green thumb, he seemed all thumbs in doing anything else. But we suggested he write to the Superintendent of Documents, U.S. Government Printing Office, Washington, D.C. 20402 for a pamphlet called "Simple Home Repairs," and at least study it. He not only did that but he also took an informal course at the retirement community on home maintenance. Jim will never be a craftsman, but he cut his home repair costs in half by learning how to do some simple home repairs. And he enjoyed it. Some community centers now have handymen who do odd jobs at a very low rate for those who cannot afford the going prices.

4. *Pool your resources.* Mary and Jim were social people, but they had never thought of cutting expenses by asking others whether or not they would like to cut costs by doing things together. They thought that their projected trips to Montana, Idaho and other places were off. But they put an ad in their community newspaper and got a lot of responses from others who wanted to make the same trip. Last year they tried with another couple and they liked it. Of course they lost privacy, but they gained fellowship. They also cut their meat bill by buying half a steer with this couple. Neither couple had room for that much meat, but by splitting it up they managed. They also began to share expenses for short trips with two other couples who were as distressed as they were over the price of gasoline.

5. *Review your investments.* The authors have recently had interviews with investment counselors about ways of fighting inflation through investments. What changes in a portfolio individuals make is determined by their life expectancy, their life-styles, and the amount they have invested. This kind of review may involve changing your

savings plan, and it should only be done in consultation with a disinterested investment counselor.

6. *Home management.* When the energy crisis first hit we were told that we might have no heating fuel in winter and no gasoline for transportation, a great to-do was made about conservation in the home. We thought it a typical putdown of the consumer, but decided, somewhat cynically, to give it a try. We monitored our lights, water, telephone and gas. To our surprise we found that in truth we had been wasteful. By using those utilities only as we needed them we cut some 30 per cent from our bills. Sometimes a postcard served instead of a long-distance phone call; sometimes a fire in the hearth made up for the chill in the house. What we are suggesitng is that all of us have been far from frugal. What started as a test of conservation ended as a hedge against inflation. With a little planning, one buying trip in the car now replaces four previous ones. Learn about the operating costs of your household and act accordingly.

7. *Earning money.* One way to replace losses from inflation is to devote some small portion of retirement time to earning money. We are not here talking about second careers. That is another subject. We are talking about earning up to the $2,400 allowed by Social Security before such earnings begin to be deducted from allocated funds. A retired professor can generally teach a night course at the university, at a junior college, or in adult education. A secretary can relieve a younger person on vacation or pregnancy leave. A retired nurse is much in demand for relief work. Part-time work is frequently possible and can be spaced so as not to encroach on life plans. For most persons this added income will partially make up for the losses from inflation and still not seriously affect their retirement plans.

These are some practical suggestions for fighting inflation. Just as important is political action to alert our elected representatives to the fact that inflation destroys us all. It would seem that this ought to be a major concern on the part of every senior citizen.

For those who are about to retire while inflation is rampant we advise seeking the aid of an experienced mathematician or statistician and let him project possible inflationary losses in terms of your projected income. It is not reasonable to assume that dollar income at retirement will mean what it once meant. For some this will mean postponing retirement; for others it will mean planning a somewhat lower level of spending; for still others it will mean more concentration of hedges against inflation. But inflation (the drop in dollar value) has become a major factor in our economic adjustment after retirement. Every person has to use his most innovative ways in coping with this problem.

Planning for Medical Emergencies

The second item on Mary and Jim's agenda was their problem with medical difficulties. We spoke in the previous chapter about various types of medical insurance and their values. But there are a great many other aspects of illness that need to be considered also. A quick look at Figure 17 will show the types of health problems that plague people over 45 years of age. Jim told us about his experience. After they had settled in the retirement community, he had fallen and fractured his hip, which required a long stay in the hospital in traction. The hospital was fifteen miles from the retirement community where they lived, and Mary could not drive. Their children lived even farther away and found it almost impossible to drive Mary to the hospital. Furthermore, she lived in such a remote suburb that it was difficult to get a bus to the hospital. This depressed her, as did living alone during that period. She finally elected to move into the home of one of their children during the duration of Jim's hospital stay. This problem of transportation is a difficult one. The retirement community had a bus that took them to their shopping center and golf course, but it did not make trips to the hospital. Also, the hospital was in a downtown area, and Mary could not find a room close to it. When Jim left the hospital he had great difficulty in being mobile. (What diseases and accidents do in restricting activity is shown in Figure 18.) Mary was not a large woman, and the problem was to help Jim move about but at the same time to keep him from falling until he had regained his strength. Jim was lonesome for home, but again it was decided that they should stay with their children until he was strong enough to function on his own. The children were glad to do this, but there were adolescents in the home; it was noisy and bustling, and the arrangement was not a happy one. Jim and Mary said that if a situation like this happened again they would try to hire a practical nurse and go to their own home; but practical nurses are hard to find and expensive. Jim and Mary's experience led us to include a "What if . . ." question in our planning with those about to be, or already, retired. These "What if . . ." questions have to do with the family and social arrangements that can be made in case of emer-

FIGURE 17

Number of Acute Conditions per 100 persons per Year, by Age, Sex,
and Condition: July 1969–June 1970

Sex and Condition Group	All Ages	Under 6 Years	6-16 Years	17-44 Years	Over 45 Years
Male					
All acute conditions	196.9	352.1	261.6	176.0	106.4
ective and parasitic diseases	24.6	53.5	40.3	17.0	9.1
piratory conditions	107.1	205.7	134.6	97.3	56.7
pper respiratory conditions	61.4	140.7	79.5	48.5	30.2
nfluenza	39.1	44.3	48.0	44.4	23.2
ther respiratory conditions	6.7	20.7	7.2	4.4	3.3
estive system conditions	10.2	10.9	15.2	9.9	6.3
uries	33.5	35.7	45.7	35.0	20.7
other acute conditions	21.5	46.3	25.8	16.9	13.6
Female					
All acute conditions	212.2	340.8	264.5	208.6	138.0
ective and parasitic diseases	24.3	57.5	34.8	22.0	9.0
piratory conditions	118.5	193.3	155.2	111.9	76.3
pper respiratory conditions	69.9	135.5	105.2	57.6	38.5
nfluenza	43.0	43.3	45.1	49.5	33.8
ther respiratory conditions	5.5	14.5	4.9	4.8	3.9
estive system conditions	11.8	14.9	16.0	11.9	7.7
uries	22.3	21.4	25.6	22.5	20.0
other acute conditions	35.3	53.8	32.8	40.4	25.0

OURCE: National Center for Health Statistics.   *Vital and Health tatistics,*   Series 10, No. 77. Washington, D.C.: U.S. Government rinting Office, 1972.

FIGURE 18

Days of Restricted Activity per Person per Year,
by Family Income, Sex, and Age (United States, 1968)

Sex and Age	All Incomes*	Family Income					
		Less than $3000	$3000–$4999	$5000–$6999	$7000–$9999	$10,000–$14,999	$15,000 or More
Male							
All ages	14.3	28.6	18.9	12.8	12.1	10.3	10.0
Under 5 years	10.9	12.6	12.4	11.3	8.5	10.6	9.0
5–14 years	9.8	11.0	8.9	9.6	10.7	9.4	9.3
15–24 years	9.7	13.3	10.3	8.8	9.7	9.2	7.9
25–44 years	11.1	24.3	18.3	11.8	10.2	7.6	9.5
45–64 years	20.6	54.9	33.4	17.1	17.7	14.5	11.0
65–74 years	31.2	42.8	31.0	25.7	27.8	16.4	18.3
75 years and over	35.0	40.9	30.9	31.8	36.9	26.1	20.4
Female							
All ages	16.3	30.6	16.9	14.5	13.1	12.9	11.4
Under 5 years	10.8	13.4	8.6	11.1	10.5	11.5	9.6
5–14 years	9.5	11.2	9.1	9.0	10.1	9.0	9.0
15–24 years	11.3	13.2	10.2	13.0	9.9	11.0	10.4
25–44 years	14.5	27.4	17.9	12.8	13.7	12.9	11.1
45–64 years	20.9	38.7	22.9	19.3	17.1	16.7	13.3
65–74 years	30.3	40.5	23.5	23.4	20.0	26.0	11.7
75 years and over	47.6	50.2	46.1	47.4	45.7	41.1	32.4

* Includes unknown income

SOURCE: National Center for Health Statistics, *Vital and Health Statistics*, Series 10, No. 67. Washington, D.C.: U.S. Government Printing Office, 1972.

gencies. And emergencies come to most of us some time or other as we grow older. A look at Figure 19 will show graphically the prevalence of chronic illnesses in older persons.

Part of the answer to the "What if . . ." questions depends on community facilities. The Shepherd Center in Kansas City furnishes older persons in that community with an effective alternative to institutional care. There is a "Telephone Alert Service" in which one can call a designated number at any hour of the day or night for emergency care. There are "Meals on Wheels" for those who for one reason or another are immobilized. There are friendly visitors who come to visit and help. There is a "Handyman" service which makes it possible to hire a handyman at a low rate to do the heavy repair work that a couple may not be able to manage. Jim and Mary would have found effective help had they lived in that locality. Other communities have organized several of these services which can be of great service to older persons during times of illness or stress. Part of a couple's effective planning is to determine what resources are available in the community and how they can be utilized. These services can be discovered by calling that person designated by the mayor to represent him for older persons, by asking at a senior citizens center, by contacting a local group of NRTA/AARP, or by speaking to a doctor or minister. There is a group of services now provided by the Federal Government's ACTION program, within the Department of Health, Education, and Welfare, that everyone needs to know about.

Much of the help that may be available is often underutilized because of lack of communication. When we were interviewing for this book we talked with one couple who were desperate because it was most difficult for them to shop. But only six blocks from their home was a senior citizens center that provided transportation to and from stores for older persons. One of the most effective ways to know what is going on locally and nationally is to join NRTA/AARP. These groups report on all programs of merit for older persons, as well as providing good reading in their magazines and bulletins. Beyond the value of information, local NRTA/AARP groups know about or may even be carrying out any number of programs such as safe-driving refresher courses, income-tax-preparation courses, consumer education, legislative advocacy programs, etc. There are entertainment meetings, educational groups, travel groups, etc. The yearly membership charge is minimal, so this investment may reap a hundredfold return. They also have a series of useful guidebooks on protection of the home, the

FIGURE 19

Some Chronic Illnesses in Older Persons
(Shown by Ten-Year Intervals)

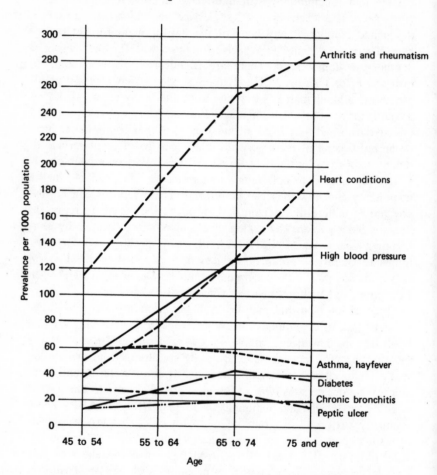

SOURCE: United States Health Survey, *Health
Statistics*, Series 6, No. 4. Washington, D.C.:
U.S. Government Printing Office, 1960.

psychology of aging, consumer education, living alone, etc., touching on almost all the problems of older persons. These booklets are free to members. There are now over seven million members of NRTA/ AARP, and these groups represent one of the strong forces in the country working for the benefit of senior citizens. In addition, there are state commissions on aging and local coordinating committees on aging that can be useful.

All of these groups depend on volunteer support. For instance, the safe-driving program and the tax information services of NRTA/ AARP are manned by almost 100,000 volunteers who are thus contributing to the improvement of the life-styles of older persons. It is increasingly common for a community to have a foster-grandparent program, a Meals-on-Wheels program, and others. Older couples who wish to add the meaning of service to their lives can explore the variety of ways they can add this other dimension to their planning. For example, Jim and Mary enjoyed their first year of retirement, but after that year they began to search for additional ways of more meaningful occupation of their time. They found it by joining AARP and taking part in their programs.

There is another major "What if . . . " that has to do with thinking about the result of total incapacitation. What if one member of the couple is so reduced in capacity as to need almost total care in an institutional setting? Discussion of nursing homes, when they become essential, is often superficial and the choice is determined by anxiety rather than by a thorough investigation. Good planning ought to include visits to, and assessments of, the available nursing homes, along with investigation of costs and conditions. It is wise to foresee such a possibility because this lets the person involved have something to say about his future. If he becomes mentally incompetent it will then be too late—one of the critical aspects of successful transitions in living arrangements for older persons is for them to have some say in the disposition of their lives. Investigations and discussions of alternatives in terms of institutional care are essential to good adjustment. Also, a decision that is made previous to need is apt to be far more satisfactory than one made under stress. Of course, as we indicated in the previous chapter, the possibility of prolonged medical care, hospitalization and nursing home care has to be included as a contingency in viable economic planning. There must always be an allowance for the unexpected. Wise life-planners include this in budgeting for the whole life span, but it becomes even more essential for the aged where the unexpected is often almost a certainty.

One of the absolute certainties is that every human being will die. There is no chance that any one of us will survive *infinitum*. We may live to be a hundred, but not two hundred. This means that planning for our last days is imperative if we are to save our family and friends from burdens they ought not be required to bear. It is sad enough to lose a life companion and to bear the inevitable burden of grief without adding the confusion of making plans for funerals, disposition of property, and financial settlements when the wishes of the deceased are not known. When someone dies without planning, there is endless waste of time, money and emotion that could have been avoided by careful preparation. The following areas of planning are essential to avoid chaos and additional sorrow.

The Funeral

A funeral of any type is a memorial to the departed. It is a way of remembering in a group the meaning that person had for life. It is an avenue for the expression of emotions that need to be felt and expressed. It is a way of bringing to those who are bereaved the resources for comfort that have been developed over thousands of years. The rituals that mankind has developed for honoring the departed also have healing aspects. The members of the group that gathers support each other and make the acceptance of death much more tolerable. For the first time there are a great many alternatives open to us as we plan for ways to express our wishes for the end.

One of the basic reasons why living persons ought to have a hand in planning their own funerals is that we reverence life, and we ought to have an opportunity to say which type of ritual marks our feelings about ourselves. In practice, we have talked with a great many individuals who have been positive about life, and a large majority of them have wanted some opportunity to have a say in the final moments of their lives on earth. So planning is essential. But planning is also important if we are to help our families avoid the excessive costs that often accrue because of a funeral. If there is no agreement that the funeral should stress relationships and life's values, it will often result in an emphasis on an expensive display. Grief is not rational, and what is done under the influence of grief is often pure waste. Funerals can cost thousands of dollars; in fact, the average cost is $1,137! That is all right if you wish your funeral to be a display, but most of us would be aggrieved to know that the family in grief felt compelled to spend that much of their limited resources. If planning is done prior to death, and the family understands what is wanted, such lavish displays will not occur.

There are several kinds of funerals possible. The standard funeral is one in which the body is embalmed, put in a casket which is present at the funeral service, and later interred in the ground or in a mausoleum. If this is to be the case and the family wishes to be interred together, it is wise to purchase enough space in the selected cemetery so that both husband and wife have peace of mind regarding their wishes long before any crisis. A simple note to survivors can indicate where that burial plot is. But there ought to be more in such a note than that information. Whatever the burial plans, it helps survivors if they know what hymns are preferred (or music, if hymns are not wanted), and what favorite passages from Scripture or poems are desired. Who should speak at the funeral? Sometimes it is a friend who has shared many experiences in the past; sometimes it is a long-time minister who has endeared himself to the family. All uncertainty about the funeral service can be eliminated by some thought before the event occurs.

There are variations on this simple funeral. Some persons like to think of a memorial service with a gathering of friends without the body or casket present. In this type of service only the family attends the interment, and a service commemorating the life of the deceased is held later—sometimes in the funeral chapel, sometimes in a church chapel, and oftentimes in the home in which the person lived. The extreme of this is the standard service where the casket is open and friends file by the body to see their friend for the last time before he is interred. Then the casket is closed and the whole group goes to the cemetery or mausoleum, where a second service is held.

In recent years a great many persons have turned to cremation as a way to dispose of the body. The ashes from cremation are then scattered in the mountains or on the sea, depending on the wishes of the departed and the laws of the state. It is possible to view the body before cremation, but this is not generally done. Most often the body is cremated and a memorial service is held without casket or body. The cost of this service is generally far below that of the cheapest funeral with casket. While there are some persons who disapprove of cremation, it should be remembered that this method is among the oldest and is found in both modern and primitive societies.

There are two organizational structures formed to help families

through the period of sorrow. There are commercial mortuaries that
have had long experience in dealing with persons in grief. They have
high overhead and their costs reflect their need to perpetuate their service. Often they are manned by understanding and friendly persons.
Recent years have seen the emergence of a second type of structure, the
cooperative memorial society. In it, the members pool their resources
and contract with someone to perform the final rites. The memorial
society is not commercial; it was formed to assist you. There is generally a nominal fee, such as $10 or $15, to join. This group exists
not only to acquaint you with the possible types of service but also to
cut the costs of death no matter whether you choose cremation or
burial in a coffin. There is a Continental Association of Funeral and
Memorial Societies, 1828 L Street, N.W., Washington, D.C. 20036
that can acquaint you with the memorial society nearest your home.

Not to be overlooked is the fact that an increasing number of persons are electing to donate various organs of their bodies in order to
bring a fuller life to people who otherwise might be blind, or without
hearing, hearts, kidneys or other organs. Or the entire body may be
donated to a medical school to help science and medical personnel
learn how to give others a fuller life. Even in death we can continue
through some of these gifts our compassion and service to others. But
provision for this must be made ahead of time, and the proper persons
must be notified.

In recent years there has been much discussion of euthanasia and
of the right to a dignified death. In a survey which the authors did in
Montana and in several areas in California, it was somewhat surprising to find over 90 per cent of all persons interviewed in these diverse
localities saying they did not want to live "beyond their years." They
explicitly stated that they wanted no "heroic methods" used to keep
them alive week after week when it had been determined by competent medical authority that their condition was such that death would
be inevitable. Each wanted to die when "my time comes." They did
not want to suffer. They asked that efforts be made to keep them comfortable as they faced their last days, but beyond that request they
did not want their doctors, their hospitals or their families to keep
them alive in a half-living state day after day. At present it is possible
to avoid those costly last weeks by the instrumentality of writing a
"Living Will," and having it witnessed by responsible parties. It does
not have the same legal standing as the better known last will and
testament, but it can direct the actions of family, minister and doctor.

The document says in simple terms that unless there is reasonable hope of recovery no extreme steps will be taken to prolong life. A copy of this Living Will should be given to a close family member, a minister, and the doctor, which will give opportunity for full discussion with each of them (see Figure 20).

Planning Your Estate

Each year a great deal of money is lost to rightful inheritors because not enough attention has been paid to ways of preserving the bulk of an estate for those who will rightfully inherit it. There are legal ways to do this in terms of predeath gifts and carefully drawn wills or trusts. Let us consider predeath gifts first. As a couple nears retirement age, they may find that they have accumulated more resources than they will ever use. In fact, their estate may be so valuable that both state and federal inheritance taxes may take a large chunk of it before those designated as recipients get their share. On the other hand, a good estate lawyer can work out a plan of yearly gifts which will enable a couple to give to those with whom they wish to share gifts amounting to no more than $3,000 a year. These are not taxable at death, so if a careful sharing plan has been worked out the estate will be much less than it would have been without those gifts. Furthermore, husbands and wives often hold on to money during the earlier years when their children really need money and then give it to them at death, when the children are already successful and do not have the need they had earlier. Couples may also give their children certain properties while they are still living. It may be to a man's advantage to deed the house to his wife. But all these possibilities must be worked out with someone who knows very clearly what the law says.

The same considerations apply to a will. It is possible to avoid an attorney's fee in some states by writing an holographic (handwritten) will entirely in one's own handwriting. We regard the procedure as risky, because without witnesses there is no one to attest to your soundness of mind when the will was written; furthermore, it could be lost; but, more importantly, it may have legal loopholes. If you, for some reason, prefer this type of will, you should still check with a lawyer to be sure that this will contains all the provisions necessary to make it legal.

We recommend that you hire a competent lawyer who can help you express all of your final wishes in a valid will, witnessed correct-

FIGURE 20
"Living Will"

NAMES AND ADDRESSES

TO MY FAMILY: _____ _____ _____
                     _____ _____ _____
                     _____ _____ _____
                     _____ _____ _____

TO MY PHYSICIAN: _____ _____ _____

TO MY CLERGYMAN: _____ _____ _____

TO MY ATTORNEY: _____ _____ _____

If the time comes when I can no longer take part in decisions for my own future
let this statement stand as the testament of my wishes:

If there is no reasonable expectation of my recovery from physical or mental
disability, I _____, _____, _____
request that I be allowed to die and not be kept alive by artificial means or
heroic measures. Death is as much a reality as birth, growth, maturity,and old
age--it is the one certainty. I do not fear death as much as I fear the indigni
ty of deterioration, dependence and hopeless pain. I ask that drugs be merciful
ly administered to me for terminal suffering even if they hasten the moment of
death.

This request is made after careful consideration. Although this document is not
legally binding, you who care for me will, I hope, feel morally bound to follow
its mandate. I recognize that it places a heavy burden of responsibility upon
you, and it is with the intention of sharing that responsibility and of miti-
gating any feelings of guilt that this statement is made.

Date: _____   Signed: _____

Witnessed by:

Signed: _____

Signed: _____

ly by two other persons, and filed with him, your conservator, and with a copy to each member of your family. The will lists your heirs, assets, your wishes, and any other final statement you may wish to make about your feelings. You must name an executor in your will. This person should be carefully chosen as a person who is trustworthy and able to see the business through. You can discuss this with your lawyer. He can also inform you of various financial arrangements through trusts which can further reduce inheritance taxes on your estate if it is sizable. We think legal consultation is a must in these circumstances.

But there is a human (and humane) side to wills that is often overlooked. In the past we have been consulted by families that have been split apart, brothers from brothers or sisters from sisters, because of conflicts resulting from the disposition of their parents' estate. This is sometimes not just a matter of money. We well remember the brother and sister who did not speak to each other for eight years (until forced to come to a reconciliation of their differences when another sister became totally incapacitated) because they each had coveted a family portrait which was left at the death of their parents. Indeed, most children have loving feelings for something in their parents' home and are bitterly disappointed if their parents do not leave them this object. Many times, however, the object they covet is money, and they may fight bitterly over the shares left to them. For this reason a fairly early family conference is quite indispensable to insure that such devastating results don't happen. By early we mean while the father and mother are still in good health and while there is time to work out any differences.

This kind of family conference is called by the father and mother to discuss the provisions of the will with their children and with any other relatives included in the will. They can use that occasion to ascertain what particular family heirlooms are coveted by what persons, what paintings, pictures or furniture is beloved by any member of the family. There may be a good deal of banter and of seeming unselfishness because of the occasion, but wise parents will discern who wants what. If there is conflict over separate items, it must be discussed and compromised. Some parents have reported their real astonishment over the passion with which their children vied for certain common possessions because they had profound meaning to the children.

Of course the will ought to be read at that time (although described as tentative) and the reactions of the family should be observed and discussed. If there is a widowed daughter who is having a difficult time making ends meet because of her children, the parents might want to give her a somewhat larger part of the estate than that given to a highly successful son who is making more money than his father ever made. Still, this ought to be thoughtfully explained, because if the will never came to light until after the parents' death, the boy might react violently—not to the differences in the amount of bequeathed money, but to the false inference that this indicated favoritism or more love for the sister. If the will is put to the family with explanations, the probabilities are that there will be no family rift or disasters. The family as a whole may have quite positive suggestions as to ways in which the will can be improved and to items that should be included which parents had never considered. Such a family council over a will leads to dignity instead of strain. It helps avoid the sniping and bickering that too readily can occur when such preparations have not been made. All of which provides poor preparation for a loving memorial service. We live in a complex world in which trusts, wills and inheritance rights have become so complicated that the average person has little competence to deal with them. Also, the commercialization of the last rites, with the many alternatives available, baffles most of us. So it is a major task to plan meaningfully in these days. Almost everyone needs the counsel of a lawyer, minister, and friends. But more important by far is sharing with the family if our heritage is to be loving memories and not bitterness. Beyond that, planning for each day and week becomes more important as we grow older. Finally, we must plan not only with an awareness of our own change but also take account of the social and economic revolution going on around us. Unless we plan in terms of our total resources, life may be devitalized. If we plan well, it can be magnificent.

9

Finding Self-Respect

A story that comes from childhood literature symbolizes the human condition as it is exacerbated by age. One of the delightful pictures many of us carry into adulthood is that of Gulliver on the island of the Lilliputians. You will remember that Gulliver fell asleep on the beach in a new land—the land of the little people. In the morning when he awakened he could not move because he was bound by ropes attached to pegs. The little people had not known what to expect from this giant and so they had secured him in absolute immobility.

Older persons themselves all too often regard themselves as being in the situation of Gulliver. Their perception of mental, psychological and physical deprivations binds them so they have no freedom. They feel that their losses deprive them of any mobility. An achievement-oriented society robs them of meaning in their daily life. The death of friends and dear ones isolates them. Economic loss cripples them.

But Gulliver escaped from his bonds. He was able to interact with the Lilliputians and convince them to trust him. In one sense older persons are like Gulliver; they are aliens in the face of the earth. Never before in history have we had such a significant number of older persons who lived beyond the fifth decade; and whose contribution to the common life has been so slight. These persons tax our economic and social resources and so society has been fearful and rejecting of them. But it may be possible, as it was for Gulliver, to escape fear and

141

encourage trust.

No one can escape history, either that of society or that of a life-time. It is true that if a relationship has been characterized by steril-ity and there is no radical intervention to stir up its elements the fu-ture will be sterile too. Individuals who have never listened with Keats to the song of a nightingale or thrilled to *Tristan und Isolde,* or min-istered to another faltering human being, or burrowed deeper and deeper into an intellectual problem, will not change their lives just by getting older. They will continue to be as unimaginative and dull as they were before. We have recounted how habit changes what could be a rewarding sexual adventure into a routinized physical exercise. The same is true about the content of our talk, our musical pursuits and our spiritual pilgrimages. It is also true that poor economic or health habits cripple our responses. All this we have said with the hope that taking stock of ourselves may lead to greater fulfillment in the last half of our lives. We have said that for the first time in history longer life, affluence and a new leisure before and in retirement give promise of exciting dimensions in living. But beyond all this there is the more basic question of the meaning of life for the older person.

The myths of yesteryear resulted in a portrait of the older person as a meaningless individual. He was defined as useless, decrepit in both body and mind, and a burden on his family and society. It is not surprising, then, that older persons became withdrawn and inert. The myths served as self-fulfilling prophecies. Research has now destroyed those myths and we have recounted that research. But the basic ques-tion of the identity and spiritual place of older persons has never been answered. In these last pages of this book we want to begin an ex-ploration into the question of the identity of the older person—who he is and what basic significance he has in his society. For after we have guaranteed economic security and health care there still remains the need for self-respect. Studies have shown that as older people give up productivity, as they move to a lower economic base, those around them degrade them. With that degradation comes a loss of self-esteem. It is at this point that we examine our culture and its relation to a new image of aging.

No man can escape history entirely, but it is possible that in the last half of his life he can escape some of its bonds. Most of us have bonds to our culture; certainly stronger than those that bound Gulliver. Those bonds in America are the products of socialization so pervasive and powerful that most of us are automatons . . . speaking and acting-out like puppets the sterile themes of the past. Endlessly striving for possessions, status, recognition, security. It is instructive to look at the curriculum served up to presidents of corporations when they take a week off for revitalization. In the curriculum there is a course on art; but it has to do with using art as a rewarding investment to bring more affluence, and not as a means of getting closer to the human soul by learning to look at life with a master. It is even more instructive to listen to the most popular television minister of the day show how spiritual approaches will result in financial success. But our possessions come to possess us, status involves conformity to the group, recognition reduces one's priorities to the mediocrity of peers, and security is bought at the price of giving up fantasy and jousting with fate. The wonder of life, the exquisite encounter with the unexpected, abandonment to play, becoming lost in the music of a waterfall or of a Beethoven sonata—all these have been abandoned; but no! they were never really experienced. The dull, daily round is incessantly performed as though we were programmed rats. As we grow older the voice loses whatever spontaneity it ever had, our spiritual vision becomes nearsighted, our world contracts. Is it strange, then, that most couples in the last half of life are bored with each other and with life? That they escape into daydreaming about those few early days which had at least some sparkle in romance and some thrill in dreams?

There is a strong possibility that the tunnel-visioned materialism that has dominated our culture takes its greatest toll on the aged who no longer can meet the norms of that *Zeitgeist*. At a time when they would like some certainty, many older people are beset by the revolutions of our day. The revolution in terms of atomic energy, in terms of sexual permissiveness, in terms of energy and mineral depletion, add to the general anxiety about aging. The world they lived in and trusted is turned upside down and the older certainties are tumbling. This generation of older persons had enough in the way of trouble in the Great Depression, the Second World War, the Korean War, and the Vietnam fiasco. Now they are faced with greater turbulence. It is not easy to find peace in a world where "all is whirl." Society fails to define aging so that older persons can feel self-respect and thus the foundations of their lives are crumbling about them.

It is this need for self-respect, for some spiritual center, for some integration of their reactions to a changing world, that is basic to any final adjustment for the senior citizen. And neither science nor religion has provided that foundation. Let us explore some of the potentials for spiritual selfhood in the late years.

Now we can explore our spiritual selves and the universe with our mates. Finally we have time to discover how the other feels about our God, our humanity and our universe. Now we should be able to talk without competing, every topic can be an avenue for self-disclosure. Our hopes for those close to us, for our community, for humanity can be shared and evaluated. The proofs we feel for immortality can be shared; the ills we have heaped on each other can be accepted and put away; until we have achieved the same intimacy of the spirit that we hope has been achieved physically. It is to be hoped that these last decades may be a time of honesty, that the defenses against each other and against the world can be abandoned, and that we can move ahead together to explore the horizons of thought and hope.

Near the end of his book on Wonder, Keen asks that we achieve the feeling that "we retain the sense of wonder which keeps us aware that ours is a holy place." We should like that to happen to married life in its final decades; that the joys of intellectual questing, aesthetic enrichment, and spiritual openness would be such that year by year we could say that "ours is a holy place," meaning that life had become so enriched by this mutual quest that our gratitude and joy could only be described by regarding it as "holy."

So we feel that intimate partnership in the later years need not be chained to dullness; it can be fulfillment provided that couples have a zest for that which is true, that which is wonderful, that which is just, and that which is beautiful.

In a book that is too little known, *Apology for Wonder,* Sam Keen has said:

> It is sometimes said that America is losing its "romantic illusions" and its spiritual heritage. The process of intellectual aging has taken over; fat has grown upon our spirits and we have ceased to be the wonder land where a man may discard the blinders of history and tradition and see with the eye of innocence.

We define senescence as a situation where there is so little joy in life that one has to run inward to the faded reminiscences of yesteryear to provide any loveliness. This is probably a valuable defense for some older persons in slums or nursing homes where there is no stimulation or beauty. We remember the old art lessons in the one-room schoolhouse many years ago where the teacher taught art appreciation by showing us a reproduction of Millet's famous painting *Man with the hoe* and then reading Edwin Markham's poem describing the man leaning on his hoe and gazing on the ground, "the emptiness of ages in his face." In this chapter we should like to explore the possibilities of finding a spiritual heritage so that older persons can love and laugh and lift up their faces to the sun.

Erik Erikson has said that our older years are the period for integration of all that we have experienced, of new spiritual horizons which order our days and give new meaning to the last decades. But all too often there is a poverty of the spirit in the last years. Our studies tell us older persons feel more need for religious undergirding in their lives than ever before but they attend church services much less. We do not wonder about this because we know that not one single denomination—Protestant, Catholic or Jewish—has ever developed a theology of aging. Only one U.S. seminary that we can identify has a single course on aging. The rationale for all this is that we are a youth-centered country and the future will be in the hands of the young people . . . except, however, that the demographers tell us that in just three decades there will be more persons over 50 years of age in this country than under the age of 50. We are an aging nation and even now much of the congregation is made up of the retired . . . and they hear no message that makes their spirits soar.

We should suppose that God is old. He existed before time itself and his Creativity goes on and will always persist. He may be timeless, but in His infinitude there is, as there is with those of us in the later years, the experience of the past. We should suppose, too, that His wisdom is accretive—that is, it grows with the generations. Robert Havighurst, that marvelous pioneer of aging studies from the University of Chicago, feels that wisdom becomes the hallmark of later years for those who adjust successfully. We like to remember the sermon preached to our forefathers on that wharf in Holland just before the *Mayflower* sailed for America in which the good pastor proclaimed that "there is still more truth to break forth from God's word." We do not assume that the minister put any limits on the age at which revelation might come to one of His children. Any theology of aging that roots itself in either the infinity of God or the progressive note of American theology would not say that there is an age limit to the discovery of new truth and deeper wisdom.

Such a theological statement would go far to nullify the youth-centeredness of our industrial and social systems, where a persistent mythology relegates older persons to the shelf of life. History itself gives the lie to that mythology, because Beethoven and da Vinci and Einstein and Michelangelo and George Bernard Shaw and . . . and . . . and . . . give contrary witness. And it has been proved in our laboratories that the vast majority of persons will be as mentally acute in their seventies and eighties as they ever were in their thirties or forties. It is true that their brains will function somewhat more slowly, but with the added ingredient of wisdom. Theologically this means that men and women can still be channels of grace, of new truth, of vast contributions to those about them. How could anyone preaching a gospel of love think that God would abandon the souls of those over 65 years old?

A second element in the theology of aging should concern *agape*. Man is called to love despite his egocentricity and his sinfulness. We have spoken a good deal about destroying the fetters on physical love of older persons; now we would like to talk about the potential of older persons for a growing sense of fellowship with all men. There is a church where this is happening. It is called Shepherd Center, and it is located in Kansas City. This Center has united Protestant, Jewish and Catholic congregations into a powerful neighborly fellowship to serve the aged.

Planned and staffed by retirees, the Shepherd Center is providing much needed support services to older people and at the same time provides opportunities to serve in meaningful activities. One of the volunteers, a retired executive, described his experience at the Center for us:

> I had always devoted much of my leisure time to volunteer work and had served on the boards of many service organizations. And I had always been a churchman. So, when I was told to begin to plan for my retirement (five years before I retired) my wife and I talked about what we would do. I decided that I wanted to do more board work and volunteer work without the restraints of my previous job. Now, what has made the difference is the removal of the restraints of work and the drains on physical and psychic energy of work. I find the Center volunteer role new in terms of human relationships, the feeling of being a part of a human chain, a lifesaving line, really, that saves the drowning on dry land. It is an adventure to find people in the community who need our help and to know you have made a difference to a fellow human being. I guess, I'm looking people in the eyes and communicating in new ways. It makes me feel alive and good inside.

One of the outcomes may not have been expected. The older persons have responded by enriching the lives of these congregations and becoming witnesses for loving concern. Their growing participation has introduced not only wisdom but also a new sense of agape into the congregation as a whole. In other communities older persons are bringing their wisdom and love to retarded children. In still others they serve as substitute families for lonely and frightened children in children's hospitals. In still others their patience and concern are helping slow readers or racially handicapped children to catch up with their more fortunate peers. All these models show that when the older person is welcomed into fellowship, the rewards are great. The admonition that we should "all be one" contains no age restriction. We should suppose that theologically older persons have a need for a life review. The oldest of our liturgies suggests that no man escapes the eternal question of life's significance. As we grow older there is time to review the course of our lives: to see that which was base and that which was noble; to settle our account. It is a time of some chagrin and of some exaltation. We would suppose that our religious conviction of forgiveness ought to help us understand that we are finite, and that to err is human—that God in his infinite understanding knows he did not create us perfect, but that we have moved toward the good life. A sensitive theological or philosophical framework ought to help us make that life review—so that when we wrap our cloak around us and lie down for our final dream it is done with ease and while at peace with our universe.

Likewise as we grow older some of the questions that plagued us as adolescents and young students come back, demanding answers. For many, these probing questions have long been avoided as too disturbing. We may be grateful for life's varied experiences, even its pain and sorrow, but still puzzled that at maturity the answers to those questions are not obvious. And many of us will be upset that just as we find some wisdom, we are called on to depart. So our thoughts become philosophical, spiritual, and sometimes more questing. We may find a new reverence for life, a new gratitude for existence, and will want to explore again the many ways in which man has tried to fathom the eternal meaning of life. So, many couples turn again to the Bible or the Torah, and find therein many of their own thoughts freshly spoken.

We suggest that it is possible to add the cultivation of wonder and awe to Erikson's theme of integration and Havighurst's stress on wisdom. There is a new element in worship these days that is called celebration. It means the gladness that comes from apprehending the total wonder of our existence. If we could break out of our defenses and our limitations wrought by possessions and fear, we might truly begin to stand in awe of the world in which we live. And that awe results in gratitude for sharing in this strange and wonderful universe so that we need to sing in gratitude. But perhaps before we can sing, we have to see our universe in new perspective. The reports of our astronauts who walked on the moon are full of wonder. The accounts of artists who have truly created a new vision are full of wonder. Poets help us escape from the prison of our little world. Working with children, who see the world freshly, sometimes helps. Sharing life's experiences with a courageous soul gives us glimpses of the unfettered response. This means that in our days of leisure we can fill our souls with substance. In our new estate of freedom we can venture on new experiences.

We may travel to see the seven wonders of the modern world, but if some circumstance prevents that, television, carefully used, can be a window on the world. We can trace the ascent of the human spirit in history with Will Durant or we can learn to look into the smallest particle of matter from the encyclopedia. All time and experience are open to us. And if we are intrigued or puzzled or entranced, we can take a course at a community college or a continuation high school. We *can* grow in wisdom, in knowledge and in grace.

Bill was 74 years old and widowed when he met Helen, who was his age. Bill had been a teacher and Helen an executive secretary. They soon found that they had the same need to fill in the gaps in their life philosophies. They could talk with animation for hours about the meaning of life and its problems. They took long trips together, but they maintained their own apartments. They often spent the entire day together because there was a genuine spiritual togetherness, but at night Bill went home. This couple never had a sexual relationship but they hugged and kissed each other. In a sense they had a spiritual marriage. When one or the other was ill, they cared for each other. The result of their "spiritual pilgrimage" together was a carefully honed philosophy of life and death. So, when Bill died it was without guilt, remorse or terror. For them, a visit to a class in religion or philosophy was as rewarding as any other kind of intimacy for others.

Of course not everyone is part of religious tradition. There are a great many persons who approach their last years with sincere agnosticism, and who would be loath to use such terms as "God" or even "spirituality." They have to find meaning in their lives without recourse to religion. But it is still possible for them to develop a sense of wonder about their existence, even though they may attribute it to chance, and they can feel gratitude about living even if they cannot reflect that gratitude to a deity. In one sense they can cope more easily or more directly with their need for identity. Religious persons have a way of repeating old theological tenets without probing. They recite verses, but as a habit rather than a cognitive experience. They may come up empty when faced with the need for identity in the later years.

Life is still a transaction between ourselves and society in the last half of life. It is important that older persons struggle like Job with the meaning of life, but it is likewise important that society change its image of aging. In a great many cultures of the past, age was venerated and the oldest person was the sage. Many biographies from that past indicate that young persons wished the years to pass quickly so that they could be old and respected as were their elders. It is difficult to believe that in a rapidly changing society such as ours older persons could have that kind of status in many sectors of our society—certainly not in science or industry. But in social and political life we sorely need the tempering influence of those who have experienced a long life. And it is probably only a dream to imagine that in a highly mobile society we will re-establish the extended family so that grandfather can direct the destiny of the clan. Still we can augment such programs as the "Grandparent Program" and give children and young people the advantage of the maturity and wisdom of older men and women. It is not a return to the past that is important. What is important is that the mass media and educational institutions begin to reflect feelings of responsibility to the aged along with gratitude for their contributions to the country.

Many older persons are banding together to work for their rights and to be witnessed as to their usefulness. Maggie Kuhn, the Gray Panther, has no lack of self-respect—she demands it from others. The legislative committees of NRTA/AARP are constantly working for better justice and recognition for the retired person. The church and the law can go far toward improving our view of aging.

There are opportunities for older persons to participate in cutting the bonds that bind them. In churches or in local political arenas they can be advocates for their peers. By being active in changing society they can find a new meaning and new self-respect. Again, they are important in the marketplaces of the country. Most older persons who begin to work for changes in the way they are treated soon start working for better conditions for others too. Nor does it take them long to discover that if we are to have political change, the kind of persons elected to office is important. So they become active in elections.

Being an advocate for a better life situation for older persons involves knowing something about the Social Security laws, pension reform, good nutrition, exercise, and so on. There is nothing so destructive as a high-powered advocate who has passion but no sense. If we are going to influence the mass media and the Federal Government we need the foundation of facts. So advocacy involves education. The least that one can ask of those who want change is that they be current in their information. One of the best signs of this in recent years is the increasing enrollment of older persons in adult education and community college classes all over the country. There they take courses that are relevant to their lives and to their communities.

There are other benefits from study. A class is a small group, and one can make friends there. Furthermore, what we learn makes it possible to be more interesting companions to our mates, friends and children. One of the first encounters in an evening class we once taught for oldsters was with an 80-year-old man who, week after week, regaled the class with denunciations of his son who was 58 years old and would not talk with him. Finally a woman, just as old as he was, spoke up and declared sharply:

> Bill, the reason you don't get to spend time with your son is that you are an old fogey—you're dumb—you don't even read the newspaper. You bore your son, just as you bore us week after week. Go to the library, read the papers and magazines and maybe even a book, and then your son will enjoy you. And forget those stories you've told all of us a dozen times.

Bill was shocked, but the rest of the group reinforced what had been said. A few weeks later he reported that he had indeed started to read, and that he and his son spent a very pleasant evening discussing current events. Something else changed about Bill, and no one quite understood why. He generally came to the group unshaven and with his shirt hanging out. He took little time to comb his hair. Maybe as his social contacts improved, his self-image improved, and consequently he reflected this in better grooming. Cleanliness may not be quite next to godliness, but it is high on the list of qualities that bring self-respect and appreciation from others.

Maintaining our sense of ethics and our consideration for others, is even more important in interpersonal relationships. The following case was reported to us by a social worker who was quite unhappy about what went on between a man and a woman:

> Martha, at 70 years of age, was an ambitious and attractive female. She ostensibly fell in love with Harry B., who then was 91 years old. They agreed to live together and did so for two years, during which time Martha had the time of her life. Harry was described as "very spry" and humorous. At the end of the two years Harry became ill, and it looked as if he might be permanently incapacitated. At that time Martha said, "No, thank you," and moved out. She found another male and moved in.

One of the dangers of companionate marriage for older persons is that there are no legal bonds. Legally, if not ethically, Martha was within her rights in moving when the fun was over. While she avoided some distress in caring for her friend, she gained the enmity of many persons around her who felt that her behavior was immoral. They had not condemned her for living with Harry. In their opinion she had entered into a contract "for better or worse," and when it got worse, she ran.

It is possible that this problem of responsibility goes beyond the aging. Given the current emphasis on hedonism, a great many younger and middle-aged persons are leaving their mates and children in search of new thrills. Watergate reminds us that utter pragmatism seems to measure norms in politics for some politicians. However, in our quest for self-respect it is important that we do not violate interpersonal responsibilities. Freedom without responsibility results in anarchy.

It is wise to make an inventory at the time of retirement of what achievements and interests have been meaningful in the past. A psychiatrist recently pointed out that recalling the "peak experiences" of the years gone by may help us relate to the activities that will be most meaningful after retirement. Discussion between partners certainly will help uncover enthusiasms long denied or perhaps forgotten. Such an inventory will also include many new opportunities for growth. It ought to include a life review so that we can come to terms with the commissions and omissions of our life. It ought to highlight our achievements and our contributions so that we can exult in them. It can help us feel the wonder of having lived at all and gratitude to all those who touched our spirit on the way. Then it ought to provide for avenues of productivity so we can use ourselves constructively so long as we live.

Gulliver, through his interactions with the little people, was freed. We feel that older persons who can realistically face the ultimate questions of life head on and not flinch and who mobilize their resources for fellowship with others can also achieve many degrees of freedom. But the rest of us also have a responsibility in making the environment conducive to the self-respect of our elders—the elders who bore us and laid the foundations of our country.

This book has tried to look honestly at the problems and opportunities for love in the later years. We have marshaled the available physiological, psychological and sociological research to destroy myths and to give a realistic picture of the problems that older persons have, both in and out of a late marriage. Most of what we reported has been positive; much has been challenging; but all has been accurate.

A final note has to be made about the progress of gerontology in the last twenty years. Before that time, scarcely any researcher was concerned with the problem of aging. We can discover none who even thought about the marital or sexual problems of those beyond fifty years of age. Now there are at least twenty gerontological centers in major universities across the country, all dedicated to finding those truths that can add joy in the aging process. At the Ethel Percy Andrus Gerontology Center at the University of Southern California some fifty scientists are at work studying aging in the single cell, as well as ways of effective intervention in the adjustment of widows. There is no significant problem which is not being scrutinized. These scientists are destroying the crippling myths about aging; and, little by little, are developing models for the good life after retirement. They need resources to continue their research and they need subjects who will cooperate in their experiments. Older couples who live near such a Center can make a vast contribution by supporting such research, both financially and with their time. Such an investment will profit the generations to come. This is another of the many suggestions made in this book to help older persons shake off apathy; to wake up and live.

But no words on paper have the power of resurrection. Our hope is to incite a great many couples, whether married or not, to assess their relationship in terms of vitality and promise. Many models are being developed to find intimacy and love, the most essential ingredients for life satisfaction and for health as we age. This book will be meaningful to you if you begin now to plan, if you make the life inventory, if you determine to seize the initiative in making life exciting instead of dreary. There are obstacles and losses, but they need not bind us so that we are inert and crippled for the rest of life.

READING REFERENCES

CHAPTER 1. *The Later Years in Fresh Perspective*

Anderson, J. E. "Psychological Aspects of the Use of Free Time." In *Free Time: Challenge to Later Maturity,* eds. Wilma Donahue, Dorothy H. Coons, and Helen K. Maurice. Ann Arbor: University of Michigan Press, 1958.

Deutsch, Helen. *Psychology of Women.* New York: Grune and Stratton, Inc., Vol. II, 1945.

Dickinson, Peter. *The Fires of Autumn.* New York: Drake Publishers, Inc., 1974.

Peterson, J. A., T. Hadwen, and A. E. Larson. *A Time for Work, A Time for Leisure: A Study of Retirement Community Inmovers.* Los Angeles: Andrus Gerontology Center, University of Southern California, 1969.

Sontag, Susan. "The Double Standard of Aging." *Saturday Review of the Society,* September 23, 1972.

CHAPTER 2. *Myth and Reality . . . in the Later Years*

Baltes, Paul B., and K. Warner Schaie. "The Myth of the Twilight Years." *Psychology Today,* March 1974, pp. 35–40.

Birren, James A., and D. W. Jeffrey. "Learning and Memory in the Mature and Learning Organism." In *The Study of Retirement and Aging.* Los Angeles: Andrus Gerontology Center, University of Southern California, 1966.

Birren, James A., and M. Bruce Fisher. "Strength and Age." *Journal of Applied Psychology* 31, p. 490. Published by the American Psychology Association, Washington, D.C.

Blood, Robert O. Jr., and Donald N. Wolfe. "Husbands and Wives." In *The Dynamics of Married Living.* Glencoe, Ill.: The Free Press, 1960.

Burgess, Ernest, and Paul Wallin. *Engagement and Marriage.* New York: Prentice-Hall, 1939.

Burr, Wesly R. "Satisfaction with Various Aspects of Marriage Over the Life Cycle" (a random middle-class sample). *Journal of Marriage and the Family* 32, February 1970.

Cuber, John F., and Peggy Harroff. *The Significant Americans*. New York: Appleton, Century, Crofts, 1965.

Leslie, Gerald R. *The Family in Social Context*. 2nd ed. New York: Oxford University Press, 1973.

Lowenthal, Marjorie Fiske, Paul L. Berkman and Associates. *Aging and Mental Disorder in San Francisco*. San Francisco: Jossey-Bass, Inc., 1967.

Peterson, J. A. *Married Love in the Middle Years*. New York: Association Press, 1968.

Pineo, Peter C. "Disenchantment in the Later Years of Marriage." In Gains in Marital Adjustment from Early to Middle Years of Marriage, on Eighteen Indices (400 couples). *Journal of Marriage and the Family,* February 1961, p. 4.

Rollins, Boyd C., and Harold Feldman. "Marital Satisfaction Over the Family Life Cycle." *Journal of Marital and Family Living* 32, No. 1, February 1970, p. 20.

CHAPTER 3. *Making the Most of the Later Years*

Angel, Robert C. *The Family Encounters the Depression*. New York: Charles Scribner's Sons, 1936.

Bernard, Jessie. "Present Demographic Trends and Structural Outcomes in Family Life Today." In *Marriage and Family Counseling,* ed. by James A. Peterson. New York: Association Press, 1968.

Cavan, Ruth S. *The American Family*. New York: Thomas Y. Crowell Co., 1953, Chapters 17, 19.

Cuber, John F., and Peggy Harroff. *The Significant Americans*. New York: Appleton, Century, Crofts, 1965.

Goode, William J. *After Divorce*. Glencoe, Ill.: The Free Press, 1956.

Hill, Reuben. "Decision Making and the Family Life Cycle." In *Social Structure and the Family: Generational Relations,* ed. by Ethel Shanas and Gordon F. Streib. Englewood Cliffs, New Jersey: Prentice-Hall, 1965.

Locke, Harvey J. *Predicting Adjustment in Marriage*. New York: Holt, Rinehart & Winston, 1951.

Neugarten, Bernice. *Middle Age and Aging*. Chicago: The University of Chicago Press, 1968.

Peterson, J. A., T. Hadwen, and A. E. Larson. *A Time for Work, A Time for Leisure: A Study of Retirement Inmovers*. Los Angeles:

Andrus Gerontology Center, University of Southern California, 1969.

Pineo, Peter C. "Disenchantment in the Later Years of Marriage." *Marriage and Family Living* 23, 1961.

CHAPTER 4. *Retirement Marriages*

Cavan, Ruth Shonle. "Speculations on Innovations to Conventional Marriage in Old Age." *The Gerontologist* 13, no. 4, Winter 1973, p. 409.

McKain, Walter C. *Retirement Marriages.* Storrs, Conn.: Storrs Agricultural Experiment Station, Monograph 3, January 1969.

Rubin, I. *Sexual Life After Sixty.* New York: Basic Books, Inc., 1965.

Shanas, Ethel, and Gordon F. Streib. *Social Structure and the Family.* Englewood, New Jersey: Prentice-Hall, Inc., 1965.

Sontag, Susan. "The Double Standard of Aging." *Saturday Review of the Society,* September 23, 1972.

CHAPTER 5. *Sexual Achievement in Marriage in the Later Years*

De Beauvoir, Simone. *The Second Sex.* Translated by H. M. Parshley. New York: Knopf, 1952.

Frank, Kenneth A., and Donald S. Kornfeld. Quoted by Stanley S. Heller in note. "Sex after Cardiac Surgery." *Medical Aspects of Human Sexuality* VIII, no. 2, February 1964.

Hastings, Donald W. *Impotence and Frigidity:* Boston: Little, Brown and Company, 1958.

Heller, Stanley S. "Sex after Cardiac Surgery." *Medical Aspects of Human Sexuality* VIII, no. 2, February 1964.

Howard, Elliott, M.D., "Tolerable Sexual Expenditure in Hypertension." In *Medical Aspects of Human Sexuality* VI, no. 2, February 1972.

Kinsey, Alfred C., Wardell B. Pomeroy and Clyde E. Martin. *Sexual Behavior in the Human Male.* Philadelphia: W. B. Saunders Company, 1948.

Kinsey, Alfred C., Wardell B. Pomeroy, Clyde E. Martin and Paul H. Gebhard. *Sexual Behavior in the Human Female.* Philadelphia: W. B. Saunders Company, 1953.

Masters, William H., M.D., and Virginia E. Johnson. *Human Sexual Response.* Boston: Little, Brown and Company, 1966. Chapters XV and XVI.

Sontag, Susan. "The Double Standard of Aging." *Saturday Review of the Society,* September 23, 1972.

CHAPTER 6.   *Sexual Achievement for the Single Person
in the Later Years*

Aging, Nos. 236–237, June-July 1974, U.S. Department of Health, Education, and Welfare, Washington, D.C.

Bernard, Jessie. "Present Demographic Trends and Structural Outcomes in Family Life Today." In James A. Peterson, ed., *Marriage and Family Counseling: Perspective and Prospect.* New York: Association Press, 1968.

Bettelheim, Bruno. *Love Is Not Enough.* Glencoe, Ill.: Free Press, 1950.

Bettelheim, Bruno. *The Empty Fortress,* New York: Free Press, 1967.

Butler, Robert N., and Myrna I. Lewis. *Aging and Mental Health.* St. Louis: Mosby Co., 1973.

Caine, Lynn. *Widow.* New York: William Morrow and Company, Inc., 1974. Quoted in *Atlanta Journal-Constitution,* Aug. 4, 1974.

Cuber, John F., and Peggy Harroff. *The Significant Americans.* New York: Appleton, Century, Crofts, 1965.

Duke University Studies in Aging. Reported in, Erdman Palmore, ed., *Normal Aging.* Durham, N.C.: Duke University Press, 1970; Erdman Palmore, ed., *Normal Aging II.* Durham, N.C.: Duke University Press, 1973.

Fromm, Erich. *Escape from Freedom.* New York: Avon, 1941.

Gesell, Arnold. *The Child from Five to Ten.* New York: Harper, 1946.

Hochschild, Arlie. *The Unexpected Community.* Englewood Cliffs, N.J.: Prentice-Hall, 1973.

Hunt, Morton. *Sexual Behavior in the 1970's.* Playboy Press, 1974.

Kassels, Victor. "Polygyny after 60." *Geriatrics* 21, no. 4, April 1966.

Kinsey, Alfred C., Wardell B. Pomeroy and Clyde Martin. *Sexual Behavior in the Human Male.* Philadelphia: W. B. Saunders Company, 1948.

Kinsey, Alfred C., Wardell B. Pomeroy, Clyde E. Martin and Paul H. Gebhard. *Sexual Behavior in the Human Female.* Philadelphia: W. B. Saunders Company, 1953.

McKain, Walter C. *Retirement Marriages.* Storrs, Conn.: Storrs Agricultural Experiment Station, Monograph 3, January 1969.

Morris, Desmond. *Intimate Behaviour.* New York: Bantam Books, 1973.

Sontag, Susan. "The Double Standard of Aging." *Saturday Review of the Society,* September 23, 1972.

CHAPTER 7. *Economics and Social Involvement*

"Developments in Aging: 1973 and January–March 1974." Report of the Special Committee on Aging, United States Senate: U.S. Government Printing Office, Washington, D.C., 1974.

Eglet, Howard. American Civil Liberties Union, quoted in "Breaking the Age Barrier." *Nation's Schools and Colleges.* September 1974, pp. 20–21.

Koffel, Norma K. Women's Equity Action League news release. *Atlanta Constitution,* August 1974.

Peterson, David. *The Crisis in Retirement Finance.* Ann Arbor, Michigan: University of Michigan, Papers in Gerontology, no. 9, 1972.

Schwartz, Arthur N., and Ivan Mensh, *Professional Obligations and Approaches to the Aged.* Springfield, Ill.: Thomas, 1974.

CHAPTER 8. *Planning for the Years Ahead*

Dynamic Maturity (NRTA/AARP magazine), 1909 K. Street, N.W., Washington, D.C., 20049.

Harmer, Ruth M. *The High Cost of Dying.* New York: Collier-Macmillan, 1963.

Hilton, John. *Dying.* New York: Penguin Books, 1969.

Modern Maturity (NRTA/AARP magazine), 1909 K. Street, N.W., Washington, D.C. 20049.

Morgan, Ernest. *A Manual of Death Education and Simple Burial.* Burnsville, N.C.: The Celo Press, 1973.

Peterson, James A. "On Being Alone." American Association of Retired Persons, Washington, D.C. 1974.

"Simple Home Repairs." U.S. Government Printing Office, Washington, D.C.

CHAPTER 9. *Finding Self-Respect*

Erikson, Erik. *Childhood and Society,* New York: W. W. Norton and Co., 1963.

Felstein, Ivor. *Living to Be a Hundred,* New York: Hippocrene Books, 1973.

Havighurst, Robert. *Developmental Tasks and Education,* 2nd ed. New York: David McKay Co., 1970.

Keen, Sam. *Apology for Wonder.* New York: Harper & Row, 1969.

INDEX